HAVEN OF LOVE AND TRUTH
Nam Sơn Trần Văn Chi
Translator: Huyền Trí

HAVEN OF LOVE AND TRUTH
Nam Sơn Trần Văn Chi
Translator: Huyền Trí

TÌNH NGHĨA GIÁO KHOA THƯ ấn bản Việt ngữ:
In ấn và phát hành tại California, Hoa Kỳ:
NXB Xưa và Nay ấn hành Lần Thứ Nhất, 2005
NXB Xưa và Nay - Tái bản - In lần Thứ Hai, 2006
NXB SỐNG - Tái bản - In lần Thứ Ba, 2024
*(Có chỉnh sửa lỗi sai sót trong 2 ấn bản 2005-2006
và thêm hình ảnh minh họa theo bài)*
Eglish Version: **HAVEN OF LOVE AND TRUTH**
SỐNG Publishing, 2024
Sách có bán trên mạng Amazon & nhà sách Tự Lực

Copyright© by Trần Văn Chi
All rights reserved
ISBN # 979-8-3304-4169-3
Library of Congress Control Number (LCCN): 2024921073

GS. Trần Văn Chi
(Chụp bởi Nhiếp Ảnh Gia Thái Đắc Nhã)
Trình bày bìa và dàn trang: Lê Giang Trần
***
Hình vẽ minh họa được sử dụng từ sách
Quốc Văn Giáo Khoa Thư
(Nha Học Chính Đông Pháp xuất bản 1935)
và một số hình ảnh sưu tầm trên mạng

Email liên lạc tác giả:
tranvannamson@gmail.com

Nam Sơn Trần Văn Chi

Translator: Huyền Trí

HAVEN OF LOVE AND TRUTH

SỐNG Publishing, 2024

Photo by Photograper Thái Đắc Nhã

Author NAM SƠN TRẦN VĂN CHI

- Born in 1943 in Gò Công province, now Tiền Giang, southern Việt Nam.
- Graduated from Saigon Pedagogical University with a major in History and Geography in 1968.
- Deputy Dean of Long Xuyên University in Southern Việt Nam until 30-4-1975.
- Activities in the Saigon Student Movement in the 70s:
  - Chairman of the Representative Board of Minh Mang University Campus.
  - Chairman of the Student Representative Board of Saigon University
  - Vice President and then Acting President of the Saigon Student Association 1967-1968

- Cultural, Social, Educational Activities:
  - Director of the Inter-School Association Adult Education Center
  - Secretary of the Inter-School Association Executive Committee until April 30, 1975
- Writing for newspapers: Thời Đại Miền Nam, Điện Tín, Tin Sáng
- Crossed the border with his family and settled in the United States from 1986 to the present:
  - Chairman and editor of the weekly magazine "Việt Nam Quê Hương" in 1994
  - Established Garment Company "V-America Inc," in Los Angeles
  - Participate in Cultural, Social, Religious, and Political activities in CaliforniaBoard of Saigon University
  - Vice President and then Acting President of the Saigon Student Association 1967-1968
- Cultural, Social, Educational Activities:
  - Director of the Inter-School Association Adult Education Center
  - Secretary of the Inter-School Association Executive Committee until April 30, 1975
  - Writing for newspapers: Thời Đại Miền Nam, Điện Tín, Tin Sáng
- Crossed the border with his family and settled in the United States from 1986 to the present:
  - Chairman and editor of the weekly magazine "Việt Nam Quê Hương" in 1994
  - Established Garment Company "V-America Inc," in Los Angeles
  - Participate in Cultural, Social, Religious, and Political activities in California

VIỆT-NAM TIỂU-HỌC TÙNG-THƯ

LECTURE (Cours préparatoires)

QUỐC-VĂN GIÁO-KHOA THƯ

(Sách tập đọc và tập viết)

LỚP DỰ-BỊ

(Sách này do Nha Học-Chính Đông-pháp đã giao cho ông TRẦN-TRỌNG-KIM, ông NGUYỄN-VĂN-NGỌC, ông ĐẶNG-ĐÌNH-PHÚC và ông ĐỖ-THẬN soạn)

NHA HỌC-CHÍNH ĐÔNG-PHÁP
XUẤT-BẢN
1935

National Literature Textbooks (Quốc Văn Giáo Khoa Thư), assigned by the Đông Pháp (Eastern French) School District, compiled by the gentlemen Trần Trọng Kim, Nguyễn Văn Ngọc, Đặng Đình Phúc, and Đỗ Thận.

Preface

NAM SƠN TRẦN VĂN CHI

LOVE AND TRUTH: MESSAGE OF THE BOOK

In 2004, I wrote a heartful book that was loved by many readers and reprinted many times, *"Love and Trust in the Textbooks,"* writing from the sources of inspiration from a series of enlightening books for primary school children created by Mr. Trần Trọng Kim's group:

National Literature Textbooks
(*Quốc Văn Giáo Khoa Thư*)

As I prepared the English version reprint of the book in 2024, I found myself again stirred by a fresh wave of inspiration. This personal journey, reigniting my passion for the book, led me to make a slight alteration in the title to reflect my renewed perspective. This change will resonate with readers who share this inspiration. I changed the title to English:

Haven of Love and Truth
(*Nơi Trú Ẩn của Tình Thương và Lẽ Thật*)

This time, we extend a special invitation to our readers. We invite you to read the book with nostalgia and emotions and delve into its deeper layers. Explore History, Geography, the Psychology of the young and old, the attitudes of invaders and oppressed people, sacrifices, and other aspects that shape our lives. Discover the different manifestations of justice and how they intersect with the paths of Love and Truth, also known as the Way.

The story still revolves around the set of National Literature Textbooks, which initially only had three small volumes, so how could it have the ability to create all kinds of magical angles? It helps transform naive children into reasonable students who know the morals of life and carry those fundamentals into life, understanding more and more until they become grayheads. As a child, I realized an infinite curiosity, a desire to know everything in life. This introductory book opened my eyes to life for the first time. It provided me with stories, history, emotions, and morality, responding to curiosity and excitement and waiting for all kinds of spirit delicacies from outside, the delicacies of Love and Truth.

Now that I have taken the slow steps of human life, walking with awareness and recognition, I can return to Love and Trust in the Teaching Textbooks. And this time, twenty years later, I discovered a new horizon. It is an open horizon, a Haven of Love and Truth.

First, we would like to invite you to take a look through the eyes of a child about the colors of this life in the excerpt from the introduction to the set of National Literature and Science Books twenty years ago:

"The first set of textbooks in Vietnamese named is the set of *National Literature Textbooks*, assigned by the Đông Pháp (Eastern French) School District, compiled by the gentlemen Trần Trọng Kim, Nguyễn Văn Ngọc, Đặng Đình Phúc, and Đỗ Thận, exclusively published by the School District, and "the state holds the copyright."

The National Literature Textbooks set includes three books:

1. *The Moral Textbook for Young Children* (*Cours Enfantin*) is a reading and writing book.
2. *The National Literature Textbooks for Preparatory Class* (*Cours Préparatoire*) is a reading book.
3. *The National Literature Textbooks for Elementary Grades* (*Cours Élémentaire*) is a reading book.

After finishing Elementary School, students go to Provincial Schools to continue studying in Second and First grades, then take the exam to obtain a Primary school Diploma.

Mr. Trần Trọng Kim (1882-1953)

***

For young people, the content of ***National Literature Textbooks*** is still somewhat relevant, and the spirit of National Literature Textbooks is something beautiful, contributing to making you "return to the source" and "preserve your originality." "ethnicity."

For the older generation, National Literature Textbooks hold enduring value. Whether you remember it vividly or as a distant memory, revisiting it fosters a more profound love for yourself and our homeland.

The moral and ethical lessons in the National Literature Textbooks have pedagogical value, contribute to human education, and are still valuable today.

***

To the younger generations, the content of the *Lecture Elementary Course* remains relevant, carrying with it a timeless beauty. It serves as a bridge to our past, guiding us to *'return to the source'* and *'preserve our national identity.'*

But as we grow older, we realize those simple ideals become increasingly challenging. The earth is getting hotter and hotter, more and more cramped. Although humans are afraid of death and suffering from war, the more scared they are, the more self-centered and selfish they become, eager to return to their primitive instinct to fight for life.

Change is not just a principle, but a force that drives all movement and evolution in history. As we delve into the history of Việt Nam and the World in *National Literature Textbooks*, we must understand that change is not a choice but a constant. Powerful nations will always seek to expand their territories, while weaker countries will always react, rise, and carve their own path. This is not just an ancient formula, but an inevitable cycle that we must accept and adapt to, for the sake of our survival and progress.

Our Việt Nam, in history, was first colonized by China and then colonized by France. Then comes the season of struggle and the domination of ideologies. Sometimes, it is hidden under the stratagem of enticement and persuasion but gradually emerges to create new, authentic, harsh methods. Which country can still rise thanks to its internal strength, not being assimilated or losing its country, thanks to cleverly adapting to the struggles between larger forces with the same concept of invasion (China, France, America, Russia, capitalism, communism, everything)? Ultimately, everything must be neutral, tolerant, and adaptive to create peace.

Right now, the world is preparing for new looks but old battles. It's an ancient tactic because it's just the basic human instinct: Greed, Anger, and Ignorance. Humans fly to the Moon and explore Mars. They did not find anything yet. Greed has to be temporarily put aside because Ignorance is still profound, and Anger is difficult to extinguish. But all is not extinguished like that. They moved on to look at other places, wherever they could conquer, they continued to find a way to proceed.

All proofs are in history. When we study history, we will see that there is the Way in history, as in life, there is the Way. The Way is the ultimate principle of life, following the correct path of evolution. Even introductory history books like the *Teaching Elementary Textbooks* have evolved religiously. Studying history is to understand the general evolution of humanity. Learning logic, philosophy, mysticism, and even science means knowing aggregation and separation, creation and destruction, causes, effects, and remedies. Learn to be human, respect, and give each other hope.

Let's return to the most fundamental principles: ***Love and Truth***, as taught in the Textbooks for preschool children. When we observe the world with a peaceful and clear mind, we realize that these principles serve as the gateway to a treasure trove of truth, the universal key to understanding humanity's movement. Despite the perpetual chaos, we are steadily progressing towards a better understanding of love, purity, and awakening.

History also shows the fusion between rulers and the ruled. There are good people among imperfect people, people who sacrifice for others to exist, people who spend their whole lives only knowing how to sacrifice and care for others, etc. That is the ultimate source of hope for the existence of humanity, of the human seeds.

Many have sacrificed themselves to contribute to their country's and humanity's future. Who are they? Temporarily call them heroic men and women, regardless of age, skin color, race, education, status, profession, career, opinion, philosophy, in the dark or the light, level degree of failure or achievement, personal or collective shortcomings. Their method of sacrifice is as resounding as thunder or as silent as the ground. They depart with a satisfied smile or tears of unfulfilled will and dreams. The common characteristics of heroic men and women are noble love, altruism, self-forgetfulness, sacrifice for the nation or humanity, courage, calmness, and disregard for life and death. They know what they need to do, and when necessary, they do not hesitate, remain calm, give their lives, and offer them to humanity, the country, others, their loved ones, or strangers.

All things are of the exact nature; they unify and interact with each other to create evolution. Each individual has yin and yang, similarities and conflicts, coordination and reaction, movement and stillness. Selfless Love and Understanding of the Truth, or Compassion and Wisdom, are the Truth, the Source of Life, and the hope for the happiness of all.

Those who are Supreme in Wisdom and Knowledge are wise, generous, and calm. The silent Saviors: Buddha, God, Bodhisattvas, Holy Spirits... They all hold the universe in the palm of their hands!

Human seeds, a metaphor for the potential and growth inherent in each individual, are born and transformed, circulating in the world and the universe. Each 'seed' must go through many reincarnations and transformations, symbolizing the journey of personal growth and evolution. They become increasingly old and strong as they mature, embodying more apparent, intelligent, and knowledgeable traits. The key is to adapt and coordinate to survive and help others survive. The 'good seeds,' 'the awakened' elders and children of one era, can grasp these things very early. We can witness this process unfolding every day. Humans are increasingly intelligent. Although many people go in the opposite direction, many glide forward to lead them onto the bright path. We will find them; look a little deeper.

That is the *Truth*; that is the *Way*. When we use Compassion and Love as our luggage and use Awakening and Wisdom to light the way, we can coordinate all human beings and put history on the right path. This emphasis on compassion, love, awakening, and wisdom is a philosophical concept and a practical guide for societal improvement. In that case, even if it takes hundreds of years, the human world will hopefully survive!

There is always a glimmer of hope for a better future!

Sincerely, Thank You, Dear Readers.

California, USA, Fall 2024

Nam Sơn Trần Văn Chi

Love and Trust in the Teaching Textbooks,
Nam Sơn Trần Văn Chi, 2006

Appreciations

NGUYỄN VĂN SÂM

THE BOOK "LOVE AND TRUST IN THE TEXTBOOKS"
and the writer's feelings about a lost time

Significantly, work carries more or less the creator's feelings; it's just that as a purely research work, the expression of emotions rarely happens. Professor Trần Văn Chi's book is not like that; it is a bridge between writing and research, so the content contains the writer's feelings. With just a quick read, readers will immediately recognize his passionate feelings for the past and his homeland on every page of the book. A past from his youth that he cherished; he found it peaceful and pure in a small homeland in his poor but cute village. This personal narrative draws readers in, making them feel part of the author's journey. What's up?

When writing the articles in this book, the author released his soul to become one with the little boy from fifty years ago. Talking about going to school on time, he spoke about how he went to school in the past, what his school bag was made of, what his ink bottle was like, what his clothes and hats were like; the story of my village school with the school drum, the classroom, and the teacher; about my memories and confide in my child when going to school. When discussing the need to love and respect teachers, he talked about the relationship between teachers and students of his time, an era when teachers were respected almost as much as their fathers; there was genuine fear and love for teachers from students, there was a day on the third day of Tết. Let the students visit the teacher's house. We encounter dozens of such cases in each of Trần Văn Chi's articles.

According to school standards, this writing style may be considered unsuitable for a heavy research book. However, in the case of Professor Trần Văn Chi's book, this unique blend of personal narrative and research is suitable and contributes to the literary genre. It is a work that bridges the gap between research and composition, and you are holding it in your hands.

Author Trần Văn Chi's approach to research and composition is unique. He stands on the research side when repeating and giving necessary details (formation and time of applying the national language, the reason for the superiority of the national language over the Vietnamese old script "Nôm." The Literary Sanctity

Temple (*V.: Văn Thánh Miếu*) in Biên Hòa and the brutal fate of this mechanism, the ancient way of telling time, the village communal house and the uses of unique places in the countryside). This approach allows him to present a comprehensive view of the topics he covers, blending personal narrative with factual information.

Although these details may not be as in-depth as the official documents from specialists we are not new to, they are enough to make the average reader excited to remember and learn a few more exciting details. When I remember, I learned a few more interesting facts.

He also uses his creative side when writing in a mixed voice, signing to express his feelings or praise something. These two aspects of writing are in harmony, mixed, and blended into gentle yet poignant articles, fun to read but valuable.

Books can help readers solve their need to learn and be an opportunity for intellectual relaxation. I like reading Trần Văn Chi because he gives me the necessary relaxation when living amid a life racing against time in a foreign country. Readers can like Trần Văn Chi, on the other hand, very cute ramblings like Queen Nam Phương's poem when he mentions: "*Each person has a homeland in their heart.*" He strayed into folk songs and activities or the history of this or that region. Those sweet folk songs, hidden in our hearts for many years, are now heard again at the right place and time... He gives us the ecstasy of saying "*our Việt people*" "*người*

Việt mình" this and that. The sound of "our Việt people" is lovely and close.

The part where he discussed the uses of the hammock was significant. It is complete yet profound and takes us into the past, into the peaceful and quiet of more than half a century ago. Readers can let their souls drift into the time of the swinging hammock (remember the poet Bàng Bá Lân). There is a sweet lullaby with the voices of my grandmother, mother, and sister.

The author's exclamations, too, sometimes make us sad. When discussing family dinners, he said: *"In the United States, some families do not value family meals. What a pity!"*.

The author's terms, *"What a pity,"* fascinate me. It's a gentle reprimand, a cry that doesn't need many words or the weight of a harsh rebuke. It signifies our shared sense of belonging, our mutual connection to the homeland, and the beautiful, time-honored customs our ancestors crafted over centuries. It's a lament for a lost past, for the cultural splendor of our people that has evolved and circumstances, yet we've managed to hold onto it.

Some of the author's most poignant words stem from his keen observations of the habits of the Vietnamese people: the pervasive tardiness at popular festival activities. When he recounted the late person's umbrella introduction: *don't see, don't care, don't listen, don't be shy*, it's clear that the author was not just embarrassed by his friend's excessive delay, but also deeply disappointed in the community's acceptance of such behavior. He felt the weight of the situation, as a member of the community.

The book consists of three parts consistent with the book series by Mr. Trần Trọng Kim, Nguyễn Văn Ngọc, Đặng Đình Phúc and Đỗ Thận. The central theme is the 'gentle and necessary morality' that teaches people *to live ethically with* the people around them and their homeland. This concept, which we now call morality, is the essential but minimum requirement to be a good person in society and the country. Unfortunately, domestic and foreign people have recently been unable to immerse themselves in this gentle and necessary morality. In some places, it is replaced by a morality that serves temporary goals, not the long-term well-being of the people and the country of Việt Nam.

Reading the book is not just a passive act but an opportunity to actively reflect on the loss of that precious social morality that should not have existed. It prompts us to consider the changes in our society and our role in preserving our cultural heritage.

While philosopher Bergson's book on two open-closed ethics holds significant intellectual value, Professor Trần Văn Chi's unique perspective on the value of feelings for the homeland and morality for society is equally essential.

As I read Professor Trần Văn Chi's book, I couldn't help but feel a personal connection. Perhaps it's because

I've absorbed the teachings of Mr. Trần Trọng Kim, Nguyễn Văn Ngọc, Đặng Đình Phúc, and Đỗ Thận, or maybe it's the familiar philosophy that seems to echo from the past. Just like how we cherish the short story A Haven of Love and Loyalty by writer Sơn Nam for its graceful repetition of sentences, this book also resonates with me.

Talking about the formation of the book, Professor Trần Văn Chi confided to me that he loved the issues raised in the book series by Mr. Trần Trọng Kim. He lived with it; he was guided by it to act in each case, such as I Shouldn't Take Revenge, I Should Be Grateful to My Teacher, My Homeland is Most Beautiful. From liking, he sought to develop it in an easy-to-follow direction so that readers would like it as much as he did, a liking that has sound effects for individuals and society. The best way is to write each installment according to your feelings, as gentle as flowing water but permeating over the long term.

I think Trần Văn Chi's book carries the good words of love. There are many repetitions and far-fetched topics, but those are shortcomings due to the necessary and lovely rambling.

Nguyễn Văn Sâm
(Rusk, days to avoid Hurricane Rita, May 10)

Appreciations

PHẠM CAO DƯƠNG

A TITLE FOR "LOVE AND TRUST IN THE TEXTBOOKS"

I had the opportunity to read and pay attention to Trần Văn Chi's series of articles since they were published in Người Việt daily newspaper, published in Orange County, California, USA, in 2004. These articles were inspired by lessons learned from a top-rated book series among Vietnamese school youth in a very ancient time, the lecture *Elementary Course* series by Mr. Trần Trọng Kim, Nguyễn Văn Ngọc, Đặng Đình Phúc, and Đỗ Thận. Attention is paid to these articles' purely emotional, literary, cultural, and educational value because the author studied at Sàigòn Pedagogical University before 1975, where I taught before emigrating to America.

Lecture Elementary Course was also used as teaching material in schools of an independent Việt Nam for a long time. The short lessons in the book are full of human love, full of images of a peaceful and gentle Việt Nam homeland, despite being colonized by foreigners before being destroyed by hatred and war; excerpts from These textbooks have been used to make dictations and translations, just enough for a lesson or an hour of study.

Trần Văn Chi's works are not written as short stories or translated into foreign languages. He was trained to be a high school History and Geography professor with a broader view of history, considering history as the entire past life of humanity, of all classes of people, not just including leaders, political activities, war, or peace. More or less living in a time when Việt Nam was not yet devastated by traumatic events. When Vietnamese people were still sincere, gentle, honest, and merciful, he wrote **Love And Trust In The Textbooks** under a vision and other content.

His works are both nostalgic and didactic, aiming to tell readers about that gentle, simple, and lovely life. He wrote as a request for himself and future generations, writing so that he could remember. If you don't write it down, it will be lost, and you won't be able to find it again because it's about a time that has passed and no longer exists.

This observation explains his writing style. Trần Văn Chi wrote ramblingly; one story followed another, and one event followed another. To use fashionable language, he wrote in a scattered manner. It started with the *Lecture Elementary Course*, annotated it, told contemporary stories, and spread overseas.

The reader is gradually led further and further away, but the goal is still the same: the same lesson has been set since the authors of the most popular Textbook set, first published in 1923, first sat down to discuss it together or just sat at the writing table.

Readers, therefore, feel energized, even though their knowledge of the people and lives of that time is not much. Everything Trần Văn Chi wrote occurred in Việt Nam less than three-quarters of a century ago. Everything until 1945 remained intact, with Trần Trọng Kim, who topped the list of authors as a pure teacher, greatly respected by everyone. His influence on Trần Văn Chi's work is significant, as it is a testament to the enduring respect for Trần Trọng Kim.

This work, *Love And Trust In The Textbooks,* should be read and worth reading, especially for young people who want to learn about Vietnamese culture and life in Việt Nam before the terrible political storms, as the Indochina War and the Việt Nam War, rushed in during the French colonial period.

Imagine the impact of this work being placed in school libraries, enriching the minds of future youth. That is not just an additional reading book, but a gateway to a deeper understanding of Vietnamese culture and history. It's a step towards a more comprehensive education system, where every school has its library and students can read more books than just a textbook, following the general evolutionary trend of all humanity.

Phạm Cao Dương

PART I

ETHIC TEACHING TEXTBOOKS

1. *Study and practice hard to become a person*
2. *What is a familial clan?*
3. *Brothers are like arms and feet*
4. *Being grateful for your parents*
5. *Obey your parents*
6. *Respect your parents*
7. *Love your parents*
8. *Ancestor worship*
9. *Choose your friend wisely*
10. *Death Anniversary*
11. *History of the country*
12. *Love others as loving yourself*
13. *Near mud but not stink of mud*

Study and practice hard to become a person
(Drawing in Lecture Elementary Course)

1. STUDY AND PRACTICE HARD TO BECOME A PERSON

In the past, our country depended on China for over a thousand years. They taught us Chinese characters, so they called them Chinese characters. Life after life, we teach each other. For a long time, I read with a Southern accent, not a Chinese accent, and my writing looked like Chinese characters. Our people's unique way of learning is called studying Confucianism. Because the way of learning at that time was intense, everyone read and taught individually. The court appointed the Principal Mandarin (Đốc Học) to manage students in each province, and the inspector Mandarin (Giám Thọ) or instructor in the prefectures and districts arranged for students to take the Multi-Province exam, selecting talented people to help the country.

When the French had not yet entered, the whole country of Six Provinces from Bình Thuận onwards had only one Gia Định exam school. Mr. Nguyễn Đình Chiểu passed the Baccalaureate in Gia Định in 1843, in the 31st year of Thiệu Trị's reign.

The Southern region of Six Provinces initially only had the Vietnamese Baccalaureate exam school in Gia Định and the Temple of Literature in Bình Dương.

In 1863, the French occupied three eastern provinces, marking a significant shift in our education system. The Grand Counselor, Sir Phan Thanh Giản, was appointed by the King as Governor of three Western provinces stationed in Vĩnh Long. By then, the Baccalaureate exam school had expanded to An Giang (Châu Đốc) and the Temple of Literature had a new branch at Long Hồ (Vĩnh Long).

When the French occupied Gia Định and then the three eastern provinces, they began to use the national language (a type of letter with the Latin letters a, b, c, transliterated in Vietnamese) to replace Chinese characters in transactions and education.

On September 18, 1924, Merlin, the governor-general of Indochina, decided to introduce the national language into teaching at the elementary level throughout Việt Nam. The School Lesson in the Moral *Teaching Textbook* is about school in the past (1924) context: ***teaching and learning the national language***.

Under the French rule in South Việt Nam, significant changes were made. The French were instrumental in establishing the village system, and constructing workhouses, elementary schools, markets, and streets.

Each Primary school usually has three Junior, Preparatory, and Senior classrooms. The school is built of bricks and tall, clean, solid tiles. It was built in a densely populated neighborhood near the markets and streets, close to the river.

The school system, a symbol of Western civilization, was a shining presence in our villages and simple, remote houses. It held significant value in winning over the hearts of the local population. The author vividly describes the school scene in the town:

> *"The clock is about to strike eight o'clock; the students are busy going to school, all five and three, checking their schoolbags, walking, and chatting happily. When they get to school, everyone goes to study; the classrooms are spacious and cool."*

At that time, students went to school twice daily, with Thursday and Sunday off. Few people owned watches.

Whatever you do, watch the rooster crow, look at the low tide, look at the sun, and guess the time. Temples have elaborate hours.

Schools have time clocks. From the French, they brought us a time-measuring device called a clock. The old clock hangs on the wall, with a "ball egg" pendulum that swings back and forth, ticking. The watch face has two hands indicating hours and minutes. The clock runs thanks to the coil. The hands of a clock rotate for 24 hours, called one day and one night, equal to the earth's rotation: 23 hours, 56 minutes, 4 seconds (rounded as 24 hours). Every hour, the clock strikes one sound (in the South, if it doesn't ring, it hits), and every 15 minutes, there is music, so it's called a musical clock.

Today, children are born seeing a clock: an alarm clock, a wristwatch, a pocket watch, etc., so they do not have the feelings of students in the Moral Teaching Textbook era.

When I was young, students went to school very early to play soccer, shuttlecock, and coolie shooting; Girls played jumping rope, playing arrows (chopsticks), and hopscotch. Hearing the drum beat three times, then three sticks, they rush back to school, lining up with sweat on their faces, still nostalgic for the game.

My Primary school when I was a child was in Tân Hòa village, the homeland of Trương Công Định's resistance war; the floor was waist high, the three steps stepped up to the surface, the main door had two enormous wings, the louver windows were wide open and bright. The roof is covered with red tiles; the floor is lined with dark red Chinese tiles. Meanwhile, the school in the neighborhood where we learned, to begin with, learning to assemble forward and backward rhymes was poor, and the teachers and students were chaotic.

The image of an ancient village school is poetic and indescribable, and perhaps each of us who has lived through it can sympathize. The peaceful childhood image under the village school with the shade of giant trees next to the village pond can no longer be found!

> *"The teacher wholeheartedly teaches you, but you should study very hard. Studying is very necessary. We have to invite each other to go to school. Only by studying can we become wise."*
>
> (Moral Teaching Textbook)

In the past, students in the South carried mat school bags, wore mat hats, and wore bà-ba shirts, short pants, and bare feet. Later, there were white student shirts, leather briefcases, and felt hats. Back then, writing paper was coarse, plain paper, and had to draw lines. Later, there were small-sized "cahier" notebooks: 32, 50, and 100 pages.

Students in the old days wrote beautifully, thanks to the teacher who taught them how to shape each stroke. They wrote with a pen and an ink nib, using purple ink to write the letters. The teachers were hardworking and role models for society, forming a close-knit community with their parents and neighbors, all invested in the children's education.

> *Without a teacher, you can't do it.*
> *If you want to go across the river, let's build a bridge,*
> *If you want a child to be literate, you must love the teacher.*

How were teachers trained back then?

Initially selected from those who passed Primary School, or if not passed, must have good handwriting. They receive a village salary or a provincial salary. Both types of rights are inferior to those of scribes and scholars, even though they come from the same background.

When the French opened a village school, people refused to let their children go because they feared the royal court or that the French would take them to the French. Therefore, the village initially forced parents to take their children to school. However, there needed to be more students for each class.

Primary school teaches and students in the classroom.
(Drawing in Lecture Elementary Course)

Concluding the article School, the authors of *"Moral Teaching Textbook"* wrote:

> *"I advise you to be diligent soon.*
> *Study and have the will to become a good person."*

Education has always been a cherished value in Vietnamese society. Despite the historical lack of formal education among Vietnamese parents, they were deeply concerned about sending their children to school, whether to learn Chinese, the national language *Nôm*, or the French language. This enduring commitment to learning underscores the high regard that our nation has always held for intellectuals and literate individuals.

> *"Students, farmers, workers, merchants"*

On the career ladder, Student (*Sĩ*) ranks first. Intellectuals and scholars are always appreciated. When it comes to social hierarchy, the teacher is second only to the King:

> *"King, Master, Father."*

Even when living abroad, the Vietnamese people's dedication to learning has continued to shine, a testament to our enduring spirit of studiousness. This commitment to education is a source of great pride for the Vietnamese people, wherever they may be.

2. WHAT IS A FAMILIAL CLAN?

The Family Lesson is the opening article about "duty towards the family" in the Moral Teaching Textbook, which is meant to be an introduction and a primer.

What is a familial clan?

"Everyone has a family, which means they have grandparents, parents, uncles, aunts, brothers, sisters. We grow up, we learn to become people, thanks to our family." (Moral Teaching Textbook)

Families are generally blood relatives, which the author has described in a way that is easy to understand, easy to remember, and easy for children to imagine. In childhood, it isn't easy to distinguish between uncles and aunts. Growing up, students will differentiate through real life: uncle is the father's younger brother, uncle is the father's older brother (speaking in the South), aunt is the father's older sister, and aunt is the mother's older sister or younger sister. The person's address seems so clear and hierarchical. In Europe and America, they need what we have. They may not have a lifestyle or structure based on family foundation but instead focus on individuality. Going abroad, the family spirit of one's family, due to circumstances, is different from that at home. But no matter what you say, Vietnamese people have had much success overseas thanks to relying on family and clan foundations.

The Moral Textbook affirmed nearly a century ago: *"We learn to become human thanks to our family."* That is still correct today, especially for people living abroad. Vietnamese parents believe that "becoming a person" does not mean turning 18 but also having a wife and husband, having children, having a house and property... Those who were fathers or mothers could share such old Vietnamese social concepts with these authors.

> *If a child surpasses his father, the family is blessed.*

In Vietnamese society, the father is always the basis for determining his children's future. So there are a few verses:

> *A child with a father is like a house with a roof,*
> *A child without a father is like a tadpole with a cut-off tail.*

The father's role is always typified and exemplary; he always shows the way for his children. (The case of President Kennedy and President Bush's family is almost similar to the Vietnamese style).

The author of Moral Textbook narrates a family as follows:

> *"My family has grandparents, parents, brothers and sisters. My father works to support the whole family. My mother cares for us, teaches us, and does the housework. We are always polite. Easy to teach, so that parents and grandparents can be happy."*

He also describes an ancient typical family in which only the father went to work. Nowadays, it's different; both parents have to work, especially in America, to take care of the family. And fortunately, Vietnamese families still have grandparents at home to look after their grandchildren, playing the role of "grandmothers."

Americans are different from us; they don't have grandmothers look after their grandchildren. Teaching

Father teaches children
(Drawing in Lecture Elementary Course)

children at home is often the mother's responsibility, so the mother dramatically influences the child's temperament, lifestyle, and behavior in general.

> *Children get spoiled by their mothers;*
> *grandchildren get spoiled by their*
> *grandmothers.*

We always teach our children to be obedient, modest, docile, and polite:

> *Fish that do not eat salt will get spoiled,*
> *Children argue with parents are naughty in*
> *hundred ways.*

Or:

> *A shirt cannot be worn over your head.*

Education in the United States encourages children to develop freely. In a multiracial and multicultural society, Vietnamese people rely on family to live, so the family is substantial.

In the conclusion, Moral Teaching Textbook goes:

> *"Even within my family are uncles, aunts,*
> *brothers, and cousins of the same blood as me."*

Families are connected by blood, that is, familial blood:

> *A drop of red blood is thicker than water.*

How precious is the relationship between family and clan? And even more precious is the Vietnamese people's love for their fellow citizens and compatriots.

But if something along the lines of "compatriots support compatriots" or "Vietnamese people vote for Vietnamese people," would that seem too much? Family spirit is good but will become narrow-minded and parochial if it is too much!

The Moral Textbook affirmed nearly a century ago: *"We learn to become human thanks to our family."* That is still correct today, especially for people living abroad. Vietnamese parents believe that "becoming a person" does not mean turning 18 but also having a wife and husband, having children, having a house and property... Those who were fathers or mothers could share such old Vietnamese social concepts with these authors.

If a child surpasses his father, the family is blessed.

In Vietnamese society, the father is always the basis for determining his children's future. So there are a few verses:

A child with a father is like a house with a roof,
A child without a father is like a tadpole with a cut-off tail.

The father's role is always typified and exemplary; he always shows the way for his children. (The case of President Kennedy and President Bush's family is almost similar to the Vietnamese style.)

The author of Moral Textbook describes a family as follows:

> *"My family has grandparents, parents, brothers and sisters. My father works to support the whole family. My mother cares for us, teaches us, and does the housework. We are always polite. Easy to teach, so that parents and grandparents can be happy."*

He also describes an ancient typical family in which only the father went to work. Nowadays, it's different; both parents have to work, especially in America, to take care of the family. Fortunately, Vietnamese families still have grandparents at home to look after their grandchildren, playing the role of "grandmothers."

Americans are different from us; they don't have grandmothers after their grandchildren. Teaching children at home is often the mother's responsibility, so the mother dramatically influences the child's temperament, lifestyle, and behavior in general.

A family with 3 generations living together in a house is typical of a clan.
(Drawing in Lecture Elementary Course)

3. BROTHERS ARE LIKE ARMS AND FEET

Our family has always consisted of grandparents, parents, and siblings. The image of the family of three generations is still present in their homeland today. That is a specific and unique feature of Vietnamese culture.

Every ancient Vietnamese family had four or more children, and it was "obligatory" for them to have a son to continue the family line and worship their ancestors. That thought seems "so old," but it is still in many people's minds. When the French occupied our country, they encouraged our people to have more children. Any family that gives birth to six or more children will be rewarded and invited to participate in "trick fights" for everyone to know. Any family that does not have children is considered unlucky and also has a sin against their ancestors.

The ancients believed that two great blessings in life were having many children and amassing wealth. These cultural values continue to resonate in Vietnamese society, connecting us to our ancestors and their beliefs.

Having an abundance of children
Having an abundance of wealth.

Having a lot of wealth means being robust and influential. And a person with many children is just as strong and influential as a person with a lot of wealth.

Raising children to adulthood is a challenging task for parents. However, an equally daunting task is instilling in them the values of love and obedience towards each other. As parents, we can understand and empathize with the worries and struggles of this responsibility.

Therefore, the Moral Teaching Textbook has the article, Brothers and Sisters. It begins with the statement: *"Siblings in the family should be harmonious and tolerant of each other, not fight or quarrel with each other so that their parents will not be upset."*

That's right, parents are distraught and unhappy when they see their children fighting and arguing.

Remember when we were children, brothers in our family often fought over food, played games, argued, and fought!

It's a common experience in many families. Parents often find themselves in the role of judges and reconcilers, having to intervene and scold to ensure their children get along.

Is discord the natural nature of a collective, even if it is a family? There must be education and advice, and there must be state law, village rules, and family law.

Bend the tree when it is young,
Teach your children when they are still innocent.

It is essential to educate people early, just like the above proverb says. Otherwise, it will take a lot of work to teach children to follow the family's rules when they grow up.

It's right. Exactly. Siblings should be tolerant of each other.

Why?

Because brothers and sisters are people of the same blood and family, they must get along and tolerate each other because of that love. That is the morality of Vietnamese people; anyone who does not keep it will be laughed at and condemned, bearing the weight of societal expectations.

Wise, homely persons are foolish in the market.
Or:

Wisely respond to outsiders,
Chickens from one mother should never fight each other.

Let's talk a little about some exciting chicken stories.

In the countryside, every house has a flock of chickens, including a rooster, many hens, and many flocks of chicks and chickens. Chickens crow to kick the hens and crow to announce the morning time. Hens give eggs and chicks. A flock of chicks over a month old, about to be separated from their mothers and about to fall apart, often fight each other. But when they grew up, they never fought each other. If you want them to fight each other, you have to smear their faces with a black pot so they don't recognize that they are from the same group, the same mother. Thus, a Vietnamese proverb says:

> *Domestic chickens smear their face to fight each other.*

It aims to inspire brothers and sisters to yield, to be harmonious, and not to compete, fostering a sense of unity and cooperation.

- Returning to the story of not having a son to carry on the family line, we recall the life of King Tự Đức. King Tự Đức (1829-1883) was the son of King Thiệu Trị and Mrs. Từ Dũ, a King who reigned for 36 years. For the Nguyễn Dynasty, he committed two major crimes (according to his belief), which were Not having a son to succeed the throne (Tự Đức was ill and had no children) and losing the country (Southern region became a French colony). If Tự Đức had a son to succeed to the throne, there would be no need for the three mandarins, Tôn Thất Thuyết, Nguyễn Văn Tường, and Trần Tiễn Thành, to overthrow the government and cause instability in the court so that the country could easily fall into French hands later (?).

Regarding the lesson that brothers and sisters must yield to each other, remember the rhyme in *Six Provinces* that you heard sung when you were a child:

Practicing the nettle plant

I, elder sister, have a husband; my young sister lives alone
I eat fish; you scoop out bones
I lie on the bed; you lie on the ground
I suck, honey; you lick the bottle
I eat sweet treat; you lick the bowl
I watch the show; you clap your hands.

What does practicing the nettle plant mean? The nettle plant (*tầm vông*) resembles bamboo but has thick flesh and a tapered trunk about an arm's length high. You can hold it so martial arts practitioners can use it. Used to practice stick techniques or as a stick and weapon without being noticed by foreigners. Thus, during the Vietnamese resistance war against the French, people used the «pointed nettle plant» to replace the spear.

The song is a perfect traditional folk piece about giving in, and it sounds humorous, but nowadays, we rarely sing it, and we don't see any books about it any more.

Brothers are like Arms and Feet

It is the conclusion of the lesson about Brotherhood.

Coming here reminds me of the Historical Story of the one sister and two brothers who were children of Marquis Nguyễn Kim, who was instrumental in restoring the Lê Dynasty. They are Ngọc Bảo (eldest sister), Nguyễn Uông, and Nguyễn Hoàng.

Nguyễn Hoàng (1524-1613): After hearing Trạng Trình's prophecy: "*Hoành Sơn one sierra - Thousand years to live.*" Then he asked his sister, Ngoc Bảo, to call for her husband Trịnh Kiểm let him go to the Southern land. Ngoc Bảo saw that her husband, Trịnh Kiểm had plotted to kill Lăng Quốc Công (Duke) Nguyễn Uông (because he was afraid that the Nguyễn family would take over his power), so she asked him to let her young brother Nguyễn Hoàng, go to govern the Southern land.

In 1558, Nguyễn Hoàng led his subordinates and relatives from Tòng Sơn district to defend Thuận Hóa. On the outside, they were friendly with the Trịnh family. Still, on the inside, they were worried about the defense, expanding their position to the South, subduing Champa, establishing Phú Yên government in 1611, and opening the way for the Southern advance.

From there, the Nguyễn Dynasty started from Gia Long and got built up. The story of the three sister and brothers, children of Nguyễn Kim, moved and changed the entire history of Việt Nam and left in our hearts a profound meaning of the saying:

> *Brothers are like hands and feet,*
> *Husband and wife are like clothes.*

A father teaches his two sons: "Brothers are like Arms and Feet"
(Drawing in Lecture Elementary Course)

In society, patience and tolerance towards outsiders have the meaning of communicating "harmoniously with disagreements" to find peace. Because there is a proverb:

'One word of tolerance, nine good words.'

Unlike familial giving, it holds particular significance for the Vietnamese community abroad, especially those experiencing family discord. The concept of tolerance within the family is unique, rooted in the love and care shared among those of the same bloodline. The patience and harmony between siblings hold deeper meanings of solidarity and strength. It's akin to the tale of a handful of chopsticks and a single chopstick. Five chopsticks together won't break; the lone chopstick will break immediately – a story that resonates with all of us from our childhood.

> *Forbear so the door and the house become good*
> *It should be rafted, tied, skidded, and beamed*

Columns, rafters, cross beams, vertical beams, and skids rely on each other to make the house stand firmly. Separated from the side of the house, they have no value in themselves.

Anyway, in reality, there are many families where women do not get along, causing family separation and so much suffering for their parents! That said:

> *Giving birth to a child, no one gives birth to a mind.*

For Vietnamese people abroad, the scene of brothers and sisters discord and not giving in to each other is not uncommon! That tragedy caused many parents to have to live alone, share a room with others, or return to Việt Nam to live alone in their homeland.

So, the Moral Teaching Textbook's lesson of Brothers and Sisters, harmony and tolerance, is meaningful and necessary. As children, we must love and tolerate each other so our parents will not be upset. When we become parents tomorrow, we will probably be upset when we see our children fighting, arguing, and discord. Life is a rotating, cyclical chain. However, as long as we are parents, everyone wants the children in the family to get along with each other.

Grandfather tells fairy tales to his grandchildren
(Lecture Elementary Course)

4. BEING GRATEFUL TO YOUR PARENTS

To teach the Junior class about the duties of children towards the family, the Moral Textbook uses two aphorisms:

Father's favor is a great mountain Thái Sơn
Mother's love is like water flowing from a source

That's the famous song *"Thankful for Parents"*. In Western society, people pay attention to politeness and learn to be courteous. Since politeness is not just a Western concept but a universal one, a convention set and agreed upon by people living together in society, how can we avoid offending each other? Therefore, Western politeness differs from Eastern morality because morality refers to "reasons, ways, boundaries to avoid bad things and follow good things" (Thanh Nghi Dictionary).

Gratitude towards parents is not just a personal duty for children in Vietnamese society; it also embodies the concept of filial piety that is deeply ingrained in our culture. This moral obligation towards our parents is a cornerstone of our society, reflecting the values of ancient Vietnamese people.

Therefore, the great Đồ Chiểu opened his famous work ***Lục Vân Tiên*** with two life-changing sentences about moral values:

> *Men take loyalty and gratitude as the lead,*
> *Girls have purity and virtue as a sentence to cultivate.*

To teach students why they should be grateful to their parents, the Textbook emphasizes: 'Parents raise children; it's a hard job, indescribable. As a child, you must know how to repay your parents' gratitude.' This responsibility is yours, as a child, to understand and fulfill.

When we were children, few people knew what it meant to be grateful to our parents, like the sky was high and the sea was vast! When we become adults, we understand some of our gratitude to our parents. Therefore, who among us does not get choked up and moved when listening to Y Van's *Mother's Heart*:

> *A mother's heart is as vast as the Pacific Ocean.*

Ancient people used the word "Thái Bình ocean" (*Pacific ocean*) to refer to something substantial and vast, just like "Thái Sơn mountain" to mention very high peaks, like parental hearts.

When we raise our children, we understand and realize how grateful we are to our parents. Nothing can be compared, measured, weighed, or counted to make it fit.

Parents in the United States raise their children very hard, but it's nothing compared to parents back home. Our Vietnamese country mothers brave the rain, wade through the water, one sun, two frosts, fasting, fasting... enduring so much pain and suffering.

That's the saying:

> *Father's favor is a high mountain Thái Sơn*
> *Mother's love is like water flowing from a source*

To show gratitude to parents, what should children do?

Moral Teaching Textbook teaches students to be grateful to their parents by being pious to them.

What is filial piety to parents?

Being filial is not just a duty; it's a way of life. It means being considerate and taking care of our parents, especially when they are sick, old, or even dead. That is the essence of filial piety.

> *The old mother lives in a thatched hut*
> *Let's visit her early and late to feel content at heart.*

The heart of filial piety lies in children's considerate attitude and affection toward their parents. Children's love and care for their parents are more precious than any material possession, gift, or money. It's a bond that transcends wealth and status. That's why we say, "The poor are filial." It's better to be poor and share and take care of your parents than to be rich, have too much money, and spend money hiring people, but not be considerate of taking care of your parents!

In the past, filial piety held immense significance, particularly for men. Sons were entrusted with the crucial tasks of maintaining the lineage, safeguarding ancestral property, tending to their grandparents' graves, and inheriting the family's wealth and legacy.

> *First is having a son; second is having a doctorate*

It sounds like we favor men and despise women, but that concept comes from the moral lifestyle and the specific life of our country in the past.

Today, that concept is still popular through the establishment of family companies in Việt Nam and the US.

For example, Trương Văn Bền et Fils is the first soap company in the Southern region, and it is Robert & Sons Inc. and Mark & Sons Company in the United States.

If in the past, men considered their daughters to be outsiders, men thought their daughters-in-law to be members of their husband's family:

> *Girls are other people's children*
> *Daughter-in-law is indeed brought home by father-mother.*

Filial piety is not heavily emphasized for the daughter-in-law. The husband's family often hopes for a gentle daughter-in-law who will give birth to children and care for the husband's family.

At weddings today, everyone wishes the couple to have a *"gentle daughter-in-law and a kind son-in-law,"* as if brides-to-be have never been kind, and every bridegroom is not kind to his wife's parents.

Returning to the Moral Textbook, in the Introduction section, the authors describe the filial child as follows:

> *"One day, Mão looked very sad when he went to school. When it was playtime, he stood in one place. The classmates played around, but he didn't care. The teacher found it strange and asked:*
>
> *What do you think that's makes you look so lost?*
>
> *Teacher, my mother fell painfully at home this morning and couldn't go to the market, so I'm sad."*

Textbook's conclusion: Mão *"is truly a filial son."*

Reading this, I remember living in the countryside with a mother and one child (my sisters were away) when I was a child. When I came home from school, I saw my mother curled up in pain in the room, so I went to the kitchen to cook porridge and bring it to her. People came in to move my mother, and she cried, making me cry, too. This story remains in my memory to this day.

Gratitude and filial piety towards parents come from shared love in the family; otherwise, it would become Western politeness.

Treat the dead as you would with the living.

That was the ancient filial piety. Even though we Vietnamese stay overseas, we still maintain those good habits. For deceased parents, the children must keep three years of mourning.

Today, while the practice of "eating vegetarian, sleeping on the floor" during mourning may have faded, the tradition of mourning for three years remains deeply ingrained in our culture. This period, marked by a temporary cessation of joyous activities, is a testament to the enduring strength of our filial piety.

In modern Vietnam history, two personalities left their careers to mourn their mother, and then their lives left a deep mark in literature and history. Even though the paths are in two different directions, opposing each other:

One was the senior teacher Nguyễn Đình Chiểu (1822-1888); at 24, he was going to Huế to participate in the Multi-Province Exam (thi Hương). When he heard that his mother had passed away, he returned to Gia Định to mourn. Loving his mother, he cried incessantly until becoming blind. Due to love for his mother and his family's destruction, he wrote the famous work *Lục Vân Tiên*.

The second figure, Mr. Trương Vĩnh Ký (1837-1898), was studying at the Pontifical Seminary (Collège

Constantine) in Poulo Pinang (Indonesia) when he received the news that his mother had passed away.

He immediately left his studies and returned to Cái Mơn to mourn her. At 21, he abandoned his monastic life and embarked on a diverse political, educational, and journalism career. However, his contribution to the discovery of the national language earned him the highest accolades, a testament to the enduring impact of his filial piety.

According to the ancient custom, when a son mourned his mother, he walked with a bamboo stick. When he mourned his father, he leaned on a walking stick (indicating a mother who is generous and easy-going with her child and a stricter father).

In Sàigòn, South Việt Nam, there was a college named after Pétrus Ký (Trương Vĩnh Ký). Following the events of 1975, Pétrus Ký School in Sàigòn was renamed, a common occurrence during this period. In contrast, Nguyễn Đình Chiểu school in Mỹ Tho still proudly retains its original name.

The remarkable filial piety demonstrated by Sirs Nguyễn Đình Chiểu and Trương Vĩnh Ký is a source of great pride. They were recognized and celebrated as two exemplary children of the Southern region.

***

Vietnamese people have been living abroad for only thirty years, and That is the first wave of migration. We certainly need to gain experience in preserving

Vietnamese identity was like Chinese identity (so that we maintain our roots). We have yet to learn enough Vietnamese. It is essential to maintain the relationship between parents and their children, protect the family structure, preserve Vietnamese identity and culture, and preserve the family foundation, including the responsibilities of children, the family, and the role models of parents for their children.

The Chinese have more experience preserving the Han identity than we do because they have had four long-standing significant migrations[1]. They know how to protect Chinese characters, as we preserve Vietnamese characters, but they preserve family rules more strictly than we do.

Children learning Vietnamese is a step in the right direction, but it's not the only thing we need. We must preserve the bond between parents and their children, protect the family structure, and uphold Vietnamese identity and culture. This includes instilling in children a sense of responsibility towards the family, a key element in preserving the family foundation.

Filial piety to parents at present as and in the past:

A son's story is like a green history.

---

1 China's four major immigration waves are:
 - Fleeing the Mongol invasion in the 13th century.
 - Fleeing the Manchu invasion in the 16th century
 - Fleeing during the fierce war that tore through China and the Japanese occupation (from the 17th to the 20th century)
 - Fleeing communism (1949)

5. OBEY YOUR PARENTS

Each Vietnamese family is a unit of society, while in Europe and America, the individual is a unit of society.

The Vietnamese family is a unique social unit bound by blood ties, a concept distinct from society's legal bindings.

This familial bond, an invisible thread connecting grandparents, parents, and children, ensures stability and sustainability. The family style, an irregular convention, dictates our interactions: eat and live together as superiors and subordinates, learn to yield, share resources, and support each other. This tradition compels us to lead respectable lives, lest we tarnish the family's reputation. For instance:

Wild child, the mother suffers.

Or:

The boat front goes astray; the helm driver bears the harm.

In Vietnamese society, the actions of an individual can have far-reaching consequences for the entire family. Whether you're a child or an adult, if you do something wrong, it's not just you who suffers the consequences. Your parents will also be discredited and laughed at by society. This collective responsibility means that from a young age, children are taught the importance of their actions and the impact they can have on their families. That is why parental education and the guidance of teachers on morality and ethics are so crucial.

The Moral Teaching Textbook of the Children class has a primer on duty towards the family and a lesson about Obedience to Parents.

I remember being a child at home; my grandparents always told me to obey my parents. Wherever I go, I listen to adults tell me to follow. When we go to school, the teacher also tells us to obey. When we grow up, get married, and become fathers and mothers, we continue to teach our children to follow from when they are toddlers, babbling to call father and mother until they grow up and become adults. Every time I disobey my grandparents or parents, I am punished by kneeling, sometimes being forced to bow my head, fold my arms, face the wall, and sometimes even be beaten. You will be rewarded with food, gifts, and outings when you obey obediently.

Why must we obey our parents?

Now, rereading it, the Moral Teaching Textbook explains:

> *"Parents are people who have experienced life and know better than truth. So if they tell us something, we must listen."*

Ah, it turns out that's it!

Parents are the ones who have gone before us, have more experience, and are more knowledgeable than us. Parents are teachers, and children must obey their parents because:

> *Fish that do not eat salt will be stinky!*

It's right. *If you argue with your parents, you will be naughty in a hundred ways*. This aphorism appeared in the context of ancient Việt Nam. The ancients did not use abstract images, conventions, or reasoning, so the aphorism *"Fish do not eat salt, rotten fish"* was readily accepted by students.

Talking about salt, remember the old days when people ate granulated salt. After that, there will be white and smooth foamy salt. However, marinating fish and making pickles often require granular salt. Our native salt is sea salt, made in Bạc Liêu, Cà Mau, Bà Rịa, Vũng Tàu... Coming to America, we eat salt from mines, like Morton Salt often sold in markets.

Returning from fishing:

> *Fish don't eat salt, rotten fish,*

and:

> *A child who argues with his parents is naughty all the way.*

Coming here, I recall the time I packed my bags and went to the province to study in second grade, away from home, when I was still playful and didn't know anything, remembering my mother's advice to study hard. At that time, I was only afraid of *making a mistake and then going a mile*. Still, I always kept to myself, suppressed my desires, fearful of making my mother sad, terrified of losing my reputation, ruining the family style, and causing scandal.

Our grandparents still know that:

> *If a child is better than a father, the family is blessed.*

However, it is normal for children to be superior to their parents in terms of school knowledge and expertise.

Let's stop here to mention that in the past, parents often arranged marriages for their children, so they taught:

> *A shirt could not be worn over the head.*

At first, it was difficult to accept because it was arbitrary and disrespectful to children. But if we consider our past society, when the agricultural society was closed, the economy was self-sufficient, and people lived in villages, what if that wasn't the case? Who would arrange the marriage for the child?

Part I
• ETHIC TEACHING TEXTBOOKS

Mother and father teache their children about good and bad person
(Lecture Elementary Course)

Nowadays, children obey their parents. If they don't, it will be difficult for them to become corrupt throughout their lives.

While styles may have evolved, the timeless wisdom of 'you wear a T-shirt that goes over your head' still holds, even in a world where children wear T-shirts that go over their heads daily!

Where is the value?

The value lies in the meaning of the saying. It reminds our children of the Lesson of Obedience because parents are more experienced than us.

King Tự Đức's story, where he was punished by his mother, Queen Mother Từ Dũ, for disobedience, serves as a powerful example of filial piety and obedience. Despite his superior royal status, his unwavering respect for his mother is a testament to the timeless lesson of obedience to parents.

> *Money is like dirt.*
> *The father eats salty food; the child is thirsty.*

Everyone has once argued with their parents, discussed with them, and even lied to them. But these experiences, though challenging, also teach valuable lessons about the importance of obeying our parents and illuminate us about the wisdom of their guidance.

Obedience to parents does not stop at moral values or because the parents have many experiences; it also starts with the children's deep love for their parents, which forms the emotional foundation of obedience.

When we were children, we studied hard, and when we grew up, we always worked and maintained our morals, not daring to commit evil deeds because we loved our parents and were afraid of making them sad.

Now read the lesson Obey Your Parents again:

> *Fish that do not eat salt will be spoiled,*
> *A child argues with his parents; he's naughty in a hundred ways.*

I'm now feeling sorry for and loving my father and mother. But unfortunately, I no longer have parents to obey!

6. RESPECT YOUR PARENTS

All children love their parents wholeheartedly, just as all parents love their children wholeheartedly. That feeling comes from blood and develops from family life.

How do we show that children love their parents?

Honestly, when we were children, no one taught us how to show that we are a child who loves our parents.

Moral Teaching Textbook teaches students that if you love your parents, you must respect them. Truly reasonable. To love each other, people must respect each other.

Children in the family always respect their parents. So what should we do to show respect for our parents?

The author proposes:

"If a child loves his parents, he will always respect them. Respect means being polite, obedient, and gentle, calling yes and yes."

Being polite means respecting your parents. When I was a child, my parents taught me to do this, do that, do this... But they rarely told me that I was polite and respected my parents.

People have always respected politeness as a measure and model to judge people.

Politeness is a way of behaving between people in the family, public places, and society, often based on age, relative rank, and social status.

Thanks to politeness, our Vietnamese family maintains hierarchy, order, and discipline, making it harmonious, happy, and sustainable: *First is politeness; Second is knowledge.*

The above proverb is always promoted in schools, engraved at the entrance gate, and solemnly written on old classrooms' molds and walls.

So, what is politeness?

First, according to the Moral Teaching Textbook, politeness is to be obedient, meaning to be easy to teach, to obey, to "call and obey."

Specifically, ancient families taught their children to say hello, talk about things, and report back. Tell adults to say yes:

The greeting was higher than the feast.

Vietnamese people value respect more than material things, gifts, and full trays.

A little person giving or taking something to an adult must do so with two hands; giving one hand is rude. In the house, the middle seat is for grandparents or parents; children are not allowed to sit. The little persons must sit below if sitting at the same table or the same set of planks.

When eating or having a party, children must always give up their chopsticks[2] and rice to adults:

Eating, watching the pot;
sitting, looking in the direction.

Children are taught to thank you when receiving gifts and apologize when they make mistakes or do things wrong. They are also taught to respect and be polite to teachers when going to school. If you want to speak in class, you have to stand up.

To read, you have to cross your arms. The teacher entered the classroom, and the students had to stand up. At the end of the hour, the students greeted the teacher and left.

Some people consider the politeness of the past "feudal." It dates back to feudal times when our country still had Kings. But feudalism does not mean overthrowing it, nor does it necessarily mean breaking it off, like Ms. Loan in Nhất Linh's work "The Break through."

Before 1975, families and schools were not the same as during the Moral Teaching Textbook, but cultural practices were still present in each family and school.

---

2 Giving up chopsticks means that younger people are polite and do not pick up food but should give rice or delicious food to older people sitting at the banquet table.

The son stands to serve his parents
(Drawing in Lecture Elementary Course)

So when going out on the street, students know to give way to the elderly and disabled; when getting on the bus, they know to give their seat to women, and if they bump into someone, they know how to apologize.

In the Introduction, there is the story of ***The Good Child***:

> *"Hợi is still young but already knows how to act like an adult. His parents love and pamper him because he is the only one. However, he never dares to be a spoiled brat. When his parents asked him anything, he replied respectfully, whatever he was told he would do immediately."*

Hợi is a polite child who everyone loves. Moral Teaching Textbook tells the story of little Hoi, the family's only son. An only child is usually a favorite; therefore, an only child is often spoiled.

Those who are only sons surely know how their parents pampered them when they were young. And if it's not damaged, it's probably due to remembering the Moral Teaching Textbook lesson.

He was looking at the drawing in the lesson on Respecting Parents, seeing the scene of Hợi standing beside his parents, reminiscing about when he was a child, remembering the old countryside scene, frugal but full of parental love. The old scenes and people, alas, are no more!!

Now, reading *Hà Nội In My Eyes* by Phạm Xuân Đài makes my heart more confused. Hà Nội, the cradle of Vietnamese culture, is a land of thousands of years of literature. Beautiful girls were there, children of good families, now belonging to history – they have changed!

People in Hà Nội today are often seen as cold, fierce, or rude, like in the movies *Hà Nội In Whose Eyes (Hà Nội Trong Mắt Ai)* and *Kindness Story (Chuyện Tử Tế)*. Have the people of Hà Nội, or the North in general, lost the core, the identity of our nation, which is the respect and politeness of the ancients?

The Southern publisher reprinted the Moral Teaching Textbook for the *Beginners class* (*Đồng Ấu*) in 1996. It was probably popularized in the North, inspiring the authors to compose the Moral Teaching Textbook. Hopefully, writer Phạm Xuân Đài will find Hà Nội people more elegant on his next visit.

Family is not just a collection of grandparents, parents, and children; more importantly, it is our relationship, treating each other as the Moral Teaching Textbook once taught us.

The spirit of respecting parents is the beauty of our culture and needs to be protected as the saying goes:
Preserve gold and pearls.

Today, in civilized times, the core of the lesson of Respecting Parents is being polite, obedient, and gentle; nothing is excessive or feudal. It represents the civilized way of Vietnamese people and is, of course, different from Western civilization.

Remembering the old days, when I came home from school, I ran back and crossed my arms to say, "Thưa bà, Thưa mẹ" *(Dear grandmother, mother - greeting means: grandma, mom, I just got back from school)* how cute it was, how precious it was!

Respecting father and mother is a good child
(Drawing in Lecture Elementary Course)

Nowadays, grandparents drive their grandchildren to school every day. Does anyone still remember anything about their school days?

The school here doesn't have the words *Before learning ritual, after learning literature* at the gate anymore. But each of us should draw that sentence in our children's hearts.

In our society, the clash of many different cultures has significant implications, underscoring the importance of preserving our cultural heritage.

The generation that learned through the Moral Teaching Textbook, now the grandparents, are passing away one by one, disappearing into oblivion.

The remaining thing is the Vietnamese family routine. Believing that "Respecting father and mother is a good child" is always valuable, so Vietnamese people in foreign countries will forever be VIETNAMESE.

7. LOVE YOUR PARENTS

Love and affection are human emotional attributes that some people consider an "instinct"?
The article Love Your Parents belongs to "duty to the family" in the Moral Teaching Textbook.

Moral Teaching Textbook opens:

> *"Parents love their children with all their heart and always worry about their children's happiness, so those who raise their children must love their parents with all their heart."*

The authors of the Moral Teaching Textbook teach, "Because our parents love us with all our hearts, as children, we must love our parents with all our hearts." That sounds like something *"quid pro quo."* They use affirmative language only to educate children.

Our past education method was to force students to accept the truth, which was very valuable for young students. However, the new process, which emphasizes the importance of love and respect, is proving even more beneficial, fostering a positive learning environment.

Throughout history, parents have always loved their children with all their heart. This love is both intuitive and sacred, beginning even before birth, not waiting until the moment of birth to take root.

Parents' love for their children grows over the years, becoming worries and concerns as they grow up.

"Making sure your children are happy" is a noble duty of parents, but it goes beyond that to become something sacred.

We, Vietnamese parents, don't tell anyone, and no school teaches us, but everyone knows how fast enough for their children to eat, have a warm, dry place to lie down and have a blanket to cover them in the cold rain.

Parents' love for their children is a selfless, enduring bond that only ends when their life ceases to breathe. It's not an exaggeration to say that Vietnamese families' love, affection, and blood ties are unique and unparalleled.

Please let me know why you say that.

We have a Vietnamese family, kinship, and village lifestyle established since ancient times.

From those events, the Moral Textbook tells students that as children, you must wholeheartedly love your parents.

Who dares to say that doing so is "reciprocity" or exchange? Then, children grow up and no longer hold their mother's hand or their father's hand. In addition to loving their parents, adult children also have other feelings growing in their hearts.

It is love, love between a boy and a girl, with an essentially sexual nature. The couple's love is more or less "possessive" and selfish. So why be afraid of losing and jealous?

Love should be good; hate should be wrong.
Love each other, love each other all the way.

The ancients had a saying, "*Husband and wife are like clothes*," meaning that husband and wife can change. This saying also meant that only the love of children and parents is eternal because that is the sacred love of blood.

Many children do not love their parents and lack their responsibilities, especially when their parents get old!

Parents raise their children like the immense sea,
Children care for parents calculate months and days.

Love must always be expressed through specific gestures and actions. If you love your teachers, you must obey them and study hard. If you love your country, you must do your duty to protect the country.

Moral Teaching Textbook uses an introduction and a story to illustrate how a child loves his parents:

> "Ti was six years old and was very playful. One day, while playing with the children, he saw his mother complain of a headache and went to bed. He stopped playing and immediately ran to touch his mother's forehead and asked:
> -What's wrong with mom?
> - Mom has a headache.
> - Let me squeeze your head to make you feel better.
> As he spoke, Ti climbed onto the bed and sat down to massage his mother's head."

The story of the Textbook is straightforward, familiar, and easy to do, aiming to train students to imitate Ti to become children who love their parents, expressed through actions.

The story of the Textbook: Ti climbed onto the bed and sat down to massage his mother's head.
(Drawing in Lecture Elementary Course)

The names Tí, Sửu, Giáp, Ất, Xuân, and Thu... refer to students in the Moral Teaching Textbook. That's also how our family named their children in the past. In the South, in six Provinces, families habitually use birth order to name their children. Like the second child, the third child, the youngest child... Some people called them *Rót, Lượm, Đâu, Đó*... like the characters in Hồ Biểu Chánh's novel.

Reading the part where Ti squeezed his mother's head reminded me of the habit in the South of "catching the wind" *(bắt gió)* every time someone has a headache. People use ginger, cumin, or *Nhị Thiên Đường* oil to rub hot on the forehead, then use two thumbs to rub, press, and pull up and down from the edge of the ears to the middle of the forehead.

In America, doctors advised against "catching the wind," but ladies still preferred "catching the wind" with green oil.

Vietnamese students often hear stories about Master Tử Lộ in China being respectful and loving to his mother. His story has been turned into a song and passed down among the people as if setting an example that all students know and listen to.

Back home, parents and children lived under the same roof, and the children were always close by to care for their parents when they were sick or in old age. It's a very normal thing to watch.

In the United States, many people see the scene of living in a nursing home and feel bored and disappointed!!

We have not yet adapted to this reality and cannot accept it. No one knows when elderly parents will be "happy" to go to a nursing home, but all parents certainly want to live with their children, especially when old age approaches.

You can if you want; if you wish to, you can't. It is truly a problem that everyone must think about, worry about, and solve.

Teach you, don't forget the words:

Loving your parents for the rest of your life is a must.

The lesson of Love Your Parents has moral value in the past and present. Practicing is difficult, especially overseas.

8. ANCESTORS WORSHIP

Vietnamese have always followed the custom of worshiping ancestors, grandparents, and parents. Wherever they go, Vietnamese families still carry that custom with them. My grandparents often said, "Wherever our children and grandchildren live, our ancestors will live there."

In the section Duties to the Family, Textbook has the article Ancestor Worship, and it begins with:

> *"Ancestors are the people who gave birth to our grandparents and parents. So, as their descendants, we must worship our ancestors to show our gratitude."*

As in the Moral Textbook and as we once told our children, grandparents give birth to parents, and parents give birth to us, and this continues from generation to generation. Each generation continues to the previous generation, making the family line continue. The national lineage is sustainable and developed to this day and into the future. Just like the proverb:

> *People have great-grandfathers and grandfathers.*
> *A tree has roots, and a river has a source.*

When we were kids, we didn't know that. Growing up, going to school, being taught by our parents, and through real life, we learn what family, clan, and nation are. That's why the Moral Teaching Textbook teaches students that we must worship our ancestors to show gratitude. It is true human morality. As the proverb goes:

> *Drinking water, remember the source.*
> *Eating fruits, remember the tree planters.*

Ancestor worship is not a religion; it is not "grandparent religious worship," as some people misunderstand and some people deliberately attribute it.

Why do you say that?

Because if we say it's a religion, there must be people who believe, people who don't think so, people who follow, and people who don't. On the other hand, worshiping ancestors expresses children's gratitude towards their grandparents. It is an obvious truth; no reasoning is needed, and no one argues. That is a good custom of our people from ancient times before religion appeared as a religion in our country.

Since when did Vietnamese people have that custom?

No one has said any affirmation. However, according to the Vietnamese spiritual book *Lĩnh Nam Trích Quái*, ancient Vietnamese people knew to call their father "Bố" (*Dad*) and mother "Cái" (*Mom*) from the time of King Lạc Long Quân, lineage surnamed Hồng Bàng. According to one of the first Vietnamese History books, *Khâm Định Việt Sử Thông Giám Cương Mục*, in year 791, Phùng Hưng, who had the merit of fighting the Tang (Đường) invaders in China, after his death was honored by the people of Sơn Tây, his homeland, as *Bố Cái Đại Vương*, considering him as their Father, Mother, and King. From then on, Vietnamese people had the custom of worshiping their parents and started calling their father "Bố" and mother "Cái".

Over time, the way Vietnamese people addressed their parents evolved. Initially, parents were also referred to as Thầy and Bu, Tia and Má, or Chú and Thím. With the influence of Western culture, the terms Dad and Mom, or Father and Mother, became more common.

From the ancient practice of respecting the dead to the modern tradition of ancestor worship, That is a journey of national civilization maturation. It's about considering the departed as still living, a spiritual continuity that bridges generations.

Death is like existence.

Many ancient houses bear the solemn inscription **'Như Tại Thế'** (*Like Existence*) on their horizontal panels, a poignant reminder to their descendants to honor and be grateful to their ancestors as if they were still among the living. This reverence for ancestors is a deeply ingrained part of Vietnamese culture, with every family having an altar to worship their grandparents.

In families in the South, in the Six Provinces region, the place of worship usually includes an altar cabinet and an altar display (for serving rice offerings). On the altar cabinet is displayed a set of three things, including an incense burner (or incense bowl); on both sides are two candlesticks to hold candles. They can also have *five things*[3] or *seven things*[4].

Behind the three-piece set are flower vases and fruit plates arranged in the "east vase, west fruit" arrangement. In front of the altar cabinet is an altar display for worship offerings.

Our family, which has five generations living together, is called the five-generation family. From the bottom up, this includes children, parents, grandparents, great-grandparents, and great-great-grandparents residing under the same roof.

How do we call each other from the fifth to the first generation?

From the fifth generation down, we call each other great-great-grandchild, great-grandchild, grandchild, child.

---

3 *Five things:* There are also two extra dishes of oil to light the lamps (in the past, coconut and peanut oil lamps were used).
4 *Seven things:* In addition to the five parts, there is an agar-wood and an incense tube.

Part I
• ETHIC TEACHING TEXTBOOKS

The woman kneels and worships at the ancestral altar.
(Painting by Trường Mỹ Thuật Gia Định, 1910-1920)

Families spanning five generations were a rarity in the past. That makes the rule set in the 7th year of Minh Mạng's reign (1826) significant. The rule was a reward for families of five generations, a feat that was not easily achieved.

These families were granted 20 taels of silver, 20 pieces of cloth, 10 pieces of silk, and 1 piece of silk, a testament to their rarity and the value placed on such familial continuity.

Nowadays, our Vietnamese family in the countryside consists of three generations: grandparents, parents, and children living together, caring for and relying on each other, which is very precious – coming to America to see that they still maintain that lifestyle is very praiseworthy.

The worship of ancestors, therefore, requires five generations, so there is the saying "five generations of great gods" (*"ngũ đại mai thần"*), which means worshiping five tablets of five generations.

In the past, tablets were often made of white Eucalyptus wood; today, they are made of regular wood, painted white, and the names of the deceased are written in black.

What happens when we worship the "five great gods" from the sixth generation onwards? Do we still worship them?

- No.

So, what happens when we reach the sixth generation and beyond in our worship of the 'five great gods'? Do we continue to worship them? The answer is no. Instead, the tablets representing these later generations are buried in the family's yard, typically near the familial worship house (*nhà từ đường*).

While this practice is less common today, with many families choosing to burn the tablets on significant days like the death anniversary or New Year's Day, the tradition of worshiping only three generations remains.

In the past, in Việt Nam, families with money and noble families left incense sticks for their descendants to take care of for worship and death anniversary offerings. The clan leader (branch leader) enjoys the portion of the "incense fire" (*hương hỏa*), including fields, gardens, land, and the worship house (*nhà từ đường*), including the belongings therein... No one can buy or sell the incense portion, including confiscation, regardless of the reason.

Ancestor worship is most solemnly held on two occasions during the year: the day of rice offering worship (death anniversary) and Tết Day.

Let's listen to the Moral Teaching Textbook talk about holidays at the worship house on the Tết holiday as follows:

> "On Lunar New Year, everyone in the family came to worship our ancestors. That day, Mr. Lý and his children went to worship their ancestors together. When they arrived at the church, Mr. Lý preached to the children: That is the worship house of "Our family lineage, to worship our ancestors, so now, on the first day of Tết, we as

grandchildren and great-grandchildren, must come to pay our respects."

Lunar New Year (*Tết Nguyên Đán*) is the most important day for all Vietnamese people: *Nguyên* is first. *Đán* is early morning. Tết begins in the Lập Xuân period, called the Spring Day.

On the first day of the New Year, they must return to the worship house, or *từ đường*, to worship their ancestors, show respect and gratitude, and pray for their ancestors to bless their descendants with happiness and longevity.

The first day, I visited my father's house.
The second day, I visited my wife's house.
On the third day, I visited my teacher's house.

In the past, Tết lasted until they took down the lucky bamboo pole Nêu (*cây Nêu*) on the seventh day. Nowadays, it is usually on the third day. That day, the family organizes offerings called "kiếu ông bà" (saying goodbye to grandparents).

During Tết, the ancestral altar is meticulously prepared, radiating solemnity and reverence. The lights, symbolizing the eternal presence of the ancestors, are kept bright throughout the three days of Tết, never to be extinguished. Tết preparations span a whole month, with children and grandchildren bringing precious gifts presented on the festival's first day, known as the procession of grandparents.

Whatever you want to offer, you must have rice, so you often hear grandparents say that you provide rice.

Offering rice on Tết must fill the bowl with a top (by placing two bowls of rice upside down). The cooked rice must be new, good, large, and not mixed with broken grains, paddy grains, grits...

The ceremony of worshiping and receiving grandparents during Tết is presided over by the clan head, traditionally the eldest son. This role underscores the significance of family hierarchy in Tết customs.

Commonly used incense offerings are 1,3,5,7... to get good luck (positive numbers), not a handful of incense like the Chinese people in Chợ Lớn that we often see. On Tết holiday, people usually use 5 or 7 fragrant incense sticks. After making three prayers, incense is placed in the incense burner, and four prostrations are made. Then come to pray. Each time you finish your vow, you must make an absolution. Then pray again. When I was a child, when I worshiped, I saw adults mumbling and shaking their lips without hearing anything!

Yes. Praying should not be said loudly to show respect and to avoid the grandparents' nicknames.

So, what is the content of the vow?

So many people don't know! According to the books, the vow includes the following:

What day is today? What ceremony would you like to celebrate? Where?

Who is the name of the person being worshiped? Who are the descendants? What do you wish for?

Descendants must kneel in front of the altar while performing worship. After pouring four levels of wine and pouring tea three times, a banquet is prepared, and we eat and drink together.

During the meal on the day of "receiving grandparents," children and grandchildren often hear stories about the family tree, industry and virtue, and their grandparents' hardships.

The lesson on ancestor worship taught students to know their roots and respect their ancestors nearly a century ago. Now, on Tết Ất Dậu, rereading it in a foreign land is so meaningful. It reminds children to worship their grandparents and ancestors because that is filial piety, not superstition. Thus, it reminds the younger generation to know their roots.

For parents, the lesson reminds us of our duty to our children. In addition to nurturing them, we must teach them to understand the beauty and goodness of their people and take care of them.

Worshipping the ancestors and expressing filial piety on the first day of the year is a beautiful and meaningful occasion. It is not superstition but an expression of respect and gratitude – a gorgeous custom or practice (*phong tục*).

The Vietnamese word for "Custom" is "*Phong Tục*," which carries particular meanings.

"Phong" and "Tục" are not just words but pillars of our culture. "Phong" is the wind of change, inviting one person and others to follow, blending in like the wind. "Tục" is the habit, the custom, the habit of imitating someone above you; you become familiar with it after a long time. Like the wind, these customs require someone to advise and guide them. They reflect the respect of the tradition, gratitude, and worship of people before us who contributed to our existence and living. That is a beautiful expression of gratitude that makes the Vietnamese people proud, and it is a beauty we should all be proud of.

In the past, when the French occupied our country, they conducted research to learn about our people's customs. There are modern intellectuals who praise, follow, and research about houses, villages, furniture, ways of dressing, sayings, beliefs, and general customs.

It's crucial to understand that Westerners study our customs not out of admiration but intending to assimilate us!

Today, we study our customs not only to see our beauty but to be proud of our nation, to remind each other, and to preserve our 'Vietnamese identity' in a foreign land. We should all take pride in our customs, which testify to our rich heritage and unique identity. That is a precious lesson from our ancestors and predecessors, and it's more important than ever in a globalized world.

Written on the occasion of Tết Ất Dậu, 2005
As a gift for fellow citizens.

9. CHOOSE YOUR FRIEND WISELY

The habit of "close to ink, you will get black."
Friends, it would help if you chose them wisely
The ones who hang out and play around
They are lazy ones; you should stay away

The above four verses, which every student of Lecture Elementary Course must know by heart, are from the article *"Choose a Friend to Play with,"* written for students around nine years old in the preparatory class.

The habit of getting close to ink to become black. Whoever you play with will be influenced by that person. Ancient ink was Chinese ink, very dark black.

Later, purple ink became popular among elementary school students. We used to cut the ink ball into pellets like pepper seeds, go to the market, buy them, soak them in hot water to dissolve, then extract them into tiny bottles to take to school. That was how we used ink in the past. But as we grew up, we saw the evolution of ink and the introduction of green and red ink. It's a journey that connects us to our past and helps us appreciate the convenience of the present.

When the French came to our country, ready-made ink sold in bottles was used to write on Parker or Kaolo pens and then on Japanese Pilot devices. Nowadays, students in the country use ballpoint pens, commonly called Bic pens (manufactured by the Bic company). In America, students use pencils very conveniently.

Ancient people often used images of daily life to educate morality in the form of folk songs and sayings such as:

> *- Near the light, it's bright.*
> *- Inside the bulb, it's round;*
> * inside the tube, it's long.*

Father teaches his son to choose friends to play with.
(Drawing in Lecture Elementary Course)

Elementary Course teaches students to choose who they want to be friends with and not pick someone promiscuous or a playboy. People who play around, hang out in the neighborhood and hang out with bad friends in groups and bands. In short, they are bad people who should not be friends.

In the realm of folklore, there exists a saying, 'fighting fish and picking melons,' a metaphor for promiscuous people, as our Course suggests. That expression, 'rolling melon,' immediately transports us to a scene where someone has stolen watermelons from the market. They patiently wait for the owner to be asleep or absent-minded, then use their feet to roll the melon out, allowing someone else to snatch it and make a quick getaway. This melon-rolling scene was a common sight at Tết markets in the areas of Cầu Ông Lãnh, Chợ Lớn Mới, or Tết markets in the Southern Province in the past.

Talking about melons, recalling the death of Mr. Nguyễn Kim, Nguyễn Hoàng's father, who first explored the South and later founded the Đàng Trong and the Lục Tỉnh (Six Provinces). He died from eating watermelon.

History records show that after Mạc Đăng Dung occupied the Lê dynasty (1527), Nguyễn Kim took his two children, Nguyễn Uông (later killed by Trịnh Kiểm, his brother-in-law) and Nguyễn Hoàng moved to Laos to restore the Lê dynasty.

After that, Nguyễn Kim brought troops back to retake Thanh Hoa and gathered many heroes to support

Lê, which caused the Mạc family to fear. So they sent the eunuch Dương Chấp Nhất, the governor of Thanh Hóa, to plot to surrender (1542). In 1545, Nguyễn Kim was killed by Dương Chấp Nhất with a poisoned melon.

Transport yourself to a time when the illustrious King Lê, in a moment of profound recognition, bestowed a title and a sacred burial place upon Nguyễn Kim in the enigmatic Tòng Sơn district. This district, steeped in legend, is said to hold a holy earth point and a dragon's jaw, a place of immense power. In this mystical setting, it was here that the descendants of Nguyễn Kim would ascend to the throne, armed with titles and military authority. His two sons, encouraged by their father's legacy, would confront the enemy in his stead, a testament to the enduring power of Nguyễn Kim's influence.

Pause momentarily to consider the profound implications of Nguyễn Kim's death. Without this pivotal event, history would have taken a dramatically different turn. Nguyễn Hoàng, for instance, would not have been compelled to seek refuge in the Southern Mountains of Hoành Sơn. The very fabric of our country's history would have been rewoven. It's a thought-provoking 'what if' scenario. It is a testament to the far-reaching consequences of a single event in history.

"Fish fighting, watermelon rolling" usually refers to nasty thieves in mediocre markets. However, "fish fighting" is also a popular game. Thus, many people like the word "fish fighting" because fish fighting is not an evil act but an exclusive diversion. Fighting fish here is a real hobby, as is playing fish fighting games. As a child in the countryside, cricket fighting and fish fighting were my favorite pastimes. Let's talk a little bit about the fish hobby.

Lia thia (or Siamese fighting fish) is a freshwater fish that only appears in the rainy season. When water floats, the fish appears in puddles next to trees and bushes in April and May of the lunar calendar. If you see a place where the water surface is foaming, use a basket to catch the fish, put it in a bottle, and cover its mouth with paper to prevent the lizard from losing it. Then, I pick up the larvae to feed them and let them fight with fish every day. from my friends in the neighborhood. What a refined pleasure!

There are two types of fish: puffer fish and fighting fish. The long-tailed puffer fish is big, extremely showy, gorgeous, and swims like a dancer but is not good at fighting. The fighting fish is slim, has a dark green body, likes to attack, and is brave. For puffer or fighting fish, only use male fish; The female fish is raised to lay eggs and give birth to babies. People catch male fish and put them in a pot of pregnant female fish so that the female can lay eggs to hatch the babies, called "pressing the fish."

That is a common occurrence among all types of male fish. They typically only fight during the mating season, driven by their instinct to compete for females.

Because male lyre fish can always fight each other, people use this characteristic to domesticate, raise, breed, and sell them to people who like to raise fish to fight each other. The Siamese lionfish (a Thai fish) is the most popular because it is brave, assertive, aggressive, and constantly attacking.

The copper fish, also known as "Indigenous fish" (*V.: cá ta*), is smaller than the Siamese fish, so the fight ends quickly, and it is not attractive to children.

In the past, in the suburbs of Sàigòn, many hamlets made a living from fishing: raising fish, pressing fish, trading fish, and catching larvae. They lived comfortably and elegantly. Watching fish fights is exciting but does not feel cruel, like watching cock fighting or buffalo fighting (in the North, it is called *"chọi trâu,"* meaning buffalo fight).

In the USA, enjoying fish fighting is quite popular, and this has created a professional fish-selling career. Fish imported from Southeast Asia include Thailand, Cambodia, Việt Nam, Malaysia, and Indonesia. Lyre fish are also called fighting fish in the US. Their scientific name is *Bettas Spendens*. Players in the US even set up an association and posted it on the Internet as an industry no worse than casinos.

More than just a pastime, fish fighting is a competitive and thrilling activity that attracts people of all ages and social levels. The more one engages in this hobby, the more they strive to improve and surpass their previous achievements, leading to a constant desire for better fish.

One of the key lessons imparted by fish fighting is the importance of choosing friends based on ethical standards. This lesson, which remains relevant today, can be applied not only to current situations but also to life in the USA. It serves as a reminder that the company we keep can significantly influence our character and values.

Briefly, choosing friends must be based on sound characters. Whether based on the criteria of "playing around" or "hardworking," choosing friends is not easy. Then, selecting friends becomes even more difficult as students grow older, change classes, change schools, and have new friends.

There are many types of friends. First, there are classmates, called classmates, peers, when they grow up, go to work, have colleagues and partners, and also have friends to hang out with, companions to go out to eat and drink. When people have money and power, they will change their tastes to suit them and, at the same time, hide their poor past. That's why there is a saying:

Rich changing friend,
Noble changing wife.

It sounds harsh, but real life is like that, although not everything.

Regarding the political arena, choosing friends and allies is far more convoluted. The process is riddled with unpredictability, leading to unexpected shifts. Consider the case of President Nixon, who once embraced Mao

Zedong during the Cold War era for strategic reasons, only to see the tables turn with Mr. Bush's current stance on China. It's as if he's aiming to restore the Han Dynasty and grant independence to previously annexed countries like Tibet, Xinjiang, and Mongolia. The only constant in this ever-changing landscape seems to be Russia.

Living in America, Vietnamese people witness a constant flux in friendships and alliances, akin to a wardrobe change. Americans believe that no one is a perpetual friend or foe. This dynamic prompts some countries to quip, 'It's better to be an enemy than an ally with America!'

This fluidity underscores the necessity for adaptability and flexibility in international relations for students and future generations in America, including our children and grandchildren.

The elementary course lecture says, "Friends should choose people." Whether based on the criteria of "playing around" or "hardworking," choosing friends is not easy. As students grow older, change classes, change schools, and have new friends, the process becomes even more complex. We all go through this journey, and understanding this can foster empathy and a deeper appreciation for the dynamics of personal relationships.

Eastern countries believe that friends must be faithful, live, and die together; betraying friends is a crime that "heaven and earth will destroy."

In the modern history of Việt Nam, in the historical stories of Vietnamese Heroes (*Đại Nam Liệt Truyện Tiền Biên*), there is a majestic, tragic story between two heroes of the period of Tây Sơn - Lord Nguyễn:

The fate is that Nguyễn Đăng Trường who worked as a Counselor of Lord Nguyễn in Thanh Hóa. When the Trịnh army invaded, he followed Prince Đông Cung Dương to Gia Định but could not make it in time, so he had to hide in Qui Nhơn with his mother.

Nguyễn Huệ knew and invited him to help, but Trường refused and asked to go to the South. Nguyễn Huệ says: "*I'm afraid there won't be enough time to repent another day,*" then let Trường follow Lord Nguyễn in the South.

Later, when he invaded Sàigòn, Nguyễn Huệ captured Nguyễn Đăng Trường and asked:

- What do you think now, sir?

Trường replied:

"Now there's only death; why bother asking?"

Nguyễn Đăng Trường was taken to the execution ground...

Choosing friends to play with has always been difficult – few people please all their friends, but everyone has friends. Choosing friends that the Elementary Course teaches students is based on "moral" standards; it seems there is no reasonable or right thing. Although it is old, it is not without any use.

10. DEATH ANNIVERSARY

Death Anniversary, also known as 'rice offering' in the South, is a reading assignment in the Lecture Elementary Course for Preparatory class. The author describes the altar on the death anniversary as follows:

> *"On the altar, the bronze and painted objects are shiny (in the shade), the candles are bright, the incense smoke is wafting, it is truly solemn."*

The death anniversary in the South is also called "rice offering."

Why do we have to hold death anniversary ceremonies and offer food to the dead?

The ancient Vietnamese custom of honoring the dead – ancestors, grandparents, parents... This custom, originating from China, where Confucius taught his students to *'Treat the dead as you would with the living,'* has evolved and transformed into a distinct 'death anniversary' custom of the Vietnamese people, a testament to the unique cultural evolution of Việt Nam.

The altar, also known as the "altar bed," is a significant part of the death anniversary ceremony in the South. Some places still use that term because, in the past, the altar was built like a bed, with a pillow on top for the deceased to rest on, symbolizing their continued presence in the family.

On the altar in the South is a set of wooden or bronze candlesticks. Between the two candlesticks is a bronze incense burner. Next to it is a vase of flowers on the right and a large plate of fruit on the left. That amalgamation of Eastern and Western elements on the altar is symbolized by the saying, *"East meets West, East pacify-West fruition,"* reflecting the cultural fusion and evolution of customs in Vietnamese culture.

Below is a procedure of ancestral worship at home:

> *"My father stood in front, lit a handful of incense, put it in the incense burner, bowed twice, then knelt with his hands clasped on his forehead, muttering a prayer. My father finished praying and bowed to the ancestors. Next, the family and we took turns bowing; each person bowed four times."*
>
> (Lecture Elementary Course)

In the North, the father is called *Thầy* (Master) or *Bố* (Daddy). In the South, he is called *Ba* (Father), and in some places, *Tía* (Pa).

Death Anniversary
(Drawing in Lecture Elementary Course)

In each family, the head of the family, a figure of authority and respect, is usually the first to worship. This act, filled with reverence, is a testament to the deep-rooted and enduring traditions of the people from Six Provinces. They bow four times at the death anniversary and make two offerings. These offerings, such as worshiping a communal house or worshiping the Lord Tomb in Bà Chiểu (*V.:Lăng Ông Bà Chiểu*), hold symbolic significance. Also, they burn three or one stick of incense instead of putting a whole handful of incense in the incense burner like the Chinese, a practice that symbolizes their unique cultural identity.

Some may wonder how many generations of death anniversary worship and ancestor worship will continue.

The answer is that these practices are not just a part of Vietnamese culture; they are its backbone. They are deeply ingrained and have stood the test of time, likely to continue for generations to come, as they serve as a way to honor and remember our ancestors.

In the South, a significant cultural practice known as the 'five elements' worship is observed. This tradition involves the celebration of the death anniversary of up to five generations. The term' five elements' refers to the five pillars of traditional Vietnamese culture – metal, wood, water, fire, and earth. After the worship, the tablet is buried, symbolizing the completion of the ritual and the continuation of the family's lineage. This unique practice not only honors the ancestors but also represents the harmony and balance of the five elements, a fundamental belief in Vietnamese culture.

Why is it called rice offering?

The term' rice offering' is used because rice holds a special place in Vietnamese culture. It is the staple food of the Vietnamese people, providing them with nourishment and sustenance. The absence of rice leads to starvation and death, highlighting its vital role in our lives.

Vital for rice, violent for money

Or:

Student first, farmer second;
When the rice runs out, the farmer first, the student second.

Ancient people held rice grains in high regard. They considered them pearls of God and believed that God would punish whoever wasted them. This belief reflects Vietnamese people's deep spiritual connection with rice, seeing it not just as a food source but as a divine gift to be cherished and respected, a symbol of life and sustenance in our culture.

In the South, the worship rituals and customs are uniquely significant. A notable aspect is the serving of four bowls of rice. Three bowls are dedicated to the deceased who have not completed their funeral rites, while five bowls are offered during the worship of 'land' or 'souls.' This rice offering is accompanied by wine and water, poured four and three times. Serving food to treat guests is delayed until the incense sticks have burned, symbolizing deep respect and reverence.

The death anniversary ceremony holds a pivotal place in the culture, as it is highly significant. A statement beautifully encapsulates the event's spirit: *'After the ceremony, the incense was exhausted, then the table on the altar was lowered, wine was served, and the whole family gathered to eat and drink happily.'*
(Lecture Elementary Course)

This statement underscores the core values of the death anniversary, highlighting the importance of remembrance, family, and celebration.

The death anniversary, a momentous occasion in the South, is a testament to the strong sense of community and togetherness. It's a time for families to come together, share delectable food, and engage in meaningful conversations. Spanning over two days, the first day is "preliminary worship," and the next is the "primary death anniversary." The death anniversary day is marked by elaborate worship and lively treatment from guests and neighbors. Some families extend their invitations to the entire hamlet or neighborhood, hosting hundreds of people to celebrate the death anniversary.

In the countryside, being invited to a death anniversary party is often called 'celebrating the death anniversary.'

On these occasions, people prepare pigs, chickens, ducks, and other delicious dishes, first as offerings and then to treat guests. This practice has given rise to a proverb: *'Eating the death anniversary meal, missing a plowing day.'* This proverb signifies the importance of these gatherings, suggesting that they are so significant that even eating can be seen as a form of work.

Every death anniversary in the countryside is a vibrant and festive affair. In preparation, the homeowner borrows tables, chairs, dishes, chopsticks, and pots and pans to entertain guests, creating a lively and bustling atmosphere. The celebration of death anniversaries or wedding parties in the countryside varies across provinces and even more in the United States. The timing of the death anniversary celebration is flexible, with the host welcoming the first ten guests to a full table, fostering a sense of joy and celebration.

The traditional menu, a testament to the rich Vietnamese culinary heritage, is a delightful array of dishes. It commences with four traditional mouthwatering starters: *Nem, Bì, Chả, Gỏi:* **Nem** (sour meatloaf), **Bì** (shredded pork skin), **Chả** (spring rolls), and **Gỏi** (sour mixed salad). That is followed by heartier fare such as curry and ragout. The grand finale is the main dish, a harmonious blend of rice and fish, a symbol of abundance and prosperity. The meal is often concluded with sweet treats like sticky rice, cakes, or bananas, which are also given as gifts for children at home.

The death anniversary is a profoundly significant event marked with solemnity and reverence. It is a poignant expression of children's gratitude toward their parents, grandparents, or ancestors. More than just a memorial, it is a time for relatives and families to reunite and for friends and neighbors to come together, fostering a sense of unity and strengthening familial and neighborly bonds.

Vietnamese people living abroad still hold to celebrate death, which is commendable. Parents rarely tell their children why they must make death anniversary offerings, so the generation born later neglects them; otherwise, they will be lost!! It's crucial that our children and grandchildren understand why they must worship on death anniversary to show filial piety, deep respect and devotion to one's parents and ancestors, and gratitude to their ancestors. If they do, they will surely appreciate the custom of death anniversary worship and help preserve it for future generations.

11. HISTORY OF THE COUNTRY

Nowadays, every country has books about that country's history. In the past, when people did not have writing, humanity generally did not have a 'written history' like today. 'Written history' refers to the recorded accounts of past events, often in books, documents, or inscriptions. To talk about history means to talk about 'written history.'

So, what is history?

- Basically, history is a record of things that have gone through.

Today, history holds a significant place in our lives. It's not just a subject taught in schools but a social science that helps us understand our past and shape our future. It's not limited to the history of a country but also encompasses the stories of individuals, like presidents and writers, and the evolution of various aspects, such as literature and fashion. For instance, the history of the car, the long dress (*áo dài*), the lady's peach bib (*yếm đào*), the Vietnamese beef soup (*phở*), the Mỹ Tho rice noodles (*hủ tiếu Mỹ Tho*), etc.

Returning to "national history" is a lesson taught to students in the past in the Lecture Course of the Preparatory class. It stated:

> *"When we study history, it's easy to know the things of the past. If we don't know how to write, we can only tell our children about the things that happened in our lives and the things that happened in the country. Words of mouth pass those stories down. So, from generation to generation, we should forget more or less, and together, we will correct them, creating fairy tales that are not true but good, so I like to tell them."*

As students, we were all captivated by the magic of historical fairy tales. With their timeless appeal, these old stories still hold us in their spell. Even today, when we recall them, it's as if we're transported back to when they first unfolded.

Let me share with you the captivating legend of Phù Đổng Thiên Vương, the Deity King of Phù Đổng. This is the tale of a courageous young boy from the village of Phù Đổng, who rode an iron horse, wielded an iron whip, and set out to conqueer the Northern Ân enemies. And then, in a twist that still baffles us, he vanished into thin air, leaving behind a legacy of bravery and heroism that still echoes through the ages.

That is the story of Sơn Tinh (a mountain divinity) and Thủy Tinh (a water divinity), with Sơn Tinh coming early to pick up the beautiful princess Mỵ Nương up Tản Viên mountain, making Thủy Tinh, who came later, angry, causing the water to rise and causing a flood.

Our country's fairy tales are vibrant. They are oral history, and while some are added or subtracted to make them more attractive, they all have actual historical elements.

Our country's history throughout ancient times, from the *Hồng Bàng family* (2879 BC to 258 BC, over 3000 years), is primarily stories; sometimes, it sounds mythical (?), lacking evidence.

During the period when we were under China, called the Northern domination period, which lasted from 111 BC to 939 AD, for over 1,000 years, our country depended on China, so Vietnamese people had a lot of Chinese influence in their culture. For a long time, we have had people who don't know our country's history as much as they know about China's history! Poetry, stories, and operas often use Chinese folk or classical stories without mentioning our good stories. Some people even criticize their history as petty compared to Chinese history!

Our past involved studying Chinese and reading Chinese books, leading to a significant influence on our culture and customs. However, our people have a unique ability to discern the beneficial aspects of Chinese culture, integrating what is suitable and discarding what is not. This discernment has evolved into our national spirit over time, showcasing our independence and cultural identity.

So, when did our country's history begin?

The written history of Việt Nam can be traced back to the Trần Dynasty in the 13th century, marking the beginning of our country's documented past. Each subsequent King who ascended the throne greatly emphasized recording his life's work, a practice known as historiography.

The first historian was Master Lê Văn Hưu from Thanh Hóa province, who passed the PhD (grade *Bảng Nhãn*, ranked second after the *Trạng Nguyên* in the Imperial exam) in 1247 at eighteen years old). He served the orders of King Trần Thánh Tông (1258-1278) and compiled the "Đại Việt History," including 30 books recording the history of our country from the Triệu dynasty (from 207 BC) to the Lý dynasty (from 1224). This handwritten history was later confiscated by the Ming (*Minh*) army and brought back to China. Although it was lost, the first set of "Đại Việt History" by Mr. Lê Văn Hưu was of great help to later historians of our country.

> *"We know history, especially because there are ancient books left behind. In many books, such as the National History Library, our ancestors recorded great deeds in Việt Nam and stories of*

great and heroic persons. Our ancestors also left inscriptions in temples, mausoleums, and steles."

(Lecture Elementary Course)

Then, more than two hundred years later, Mr. Ngô Sĩ Liên, at the behest of King Lê Thánh Tôn, compiled the Complete History of Đại Việt (*Đại Việt Sử Ký Toàn Thư*) with 15 volumes, including five volumes from the time of King Hồng Bàng to the end of Chinese dependence (939). It is called the Outer Part (*Ngoại Kỷ*).

During the French occupation, they delved into our country's history, studying ancient autographs and relics of historical nature in architectural works such as pagodas, mausoleums, village communal houses, ancient tombs, and ancient coins. These relics, our cultural heritage, are the tangible evidence that helps us and the world understand more about Việt Nam. They are the keys to our past, and from there, they become interested in researching and recording the country's history.

Mr. Trần Trọng Kim is the first Vietnamese intellectual to research the country's history in the French way and write the "Việt Nam Brief History" (*Việt Nam Sử Lược*). Although it is a "brief history," it is still considered an essential resource for researchers of the country's history.

Nowadays, every country values its history. For us, overseas Vietnamese, teaching our children to understand our history is even more critical. Why is speaking even more important?

Understanding history is about more than just knowing facts. It's about understanding how our ancestors lived and sacrificed to leave the nation a country, an S-shaped stretch of Việt Nam running along the Pacific Ocean. Our country has a position on earth, under the sun today, thanks to the merits of our ancestors.

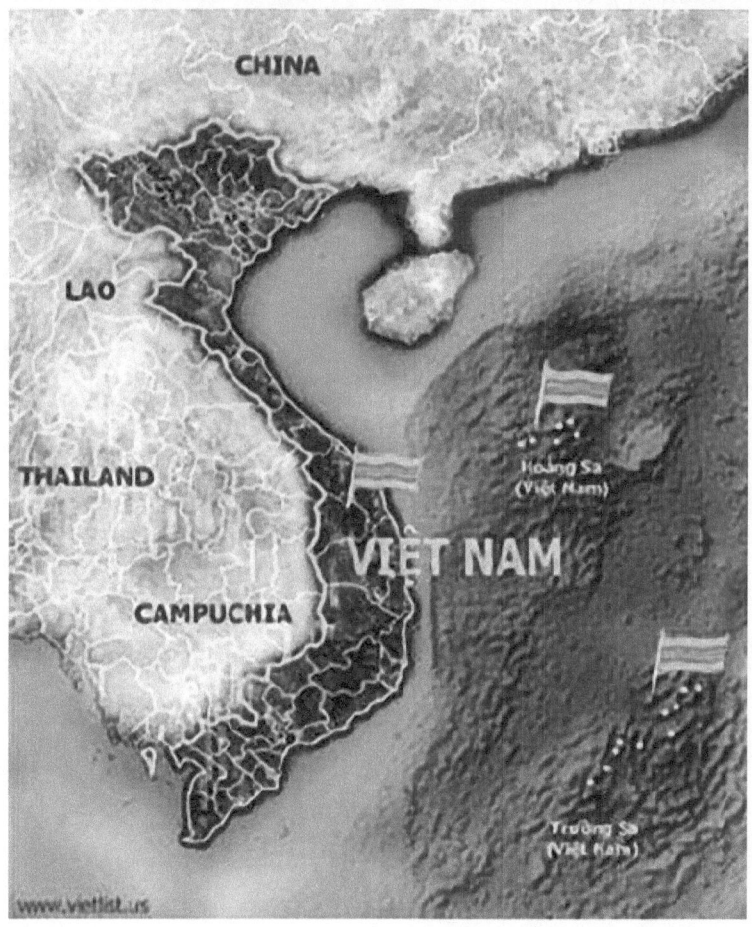

Việt Nam map includes 2 archipelagos Hoàng Sa and Trường Sa.

By understanding the efforts of our ancestors, our children and grandchildren will have a deep sense of patriotism and respect for their heritage.

Recently, there was a story about a student in a literature class in Hà Nội, Nguyễn Phi Thanh, intentionally going off-topic and reacting to the essay exam: "Please introduce the beauty of in the *Oration to the Sacrificed Fighters of Cần Giuộc*" (Văn Tế Nghĩa Sĩ Cần Giuộc) by Nguyễn Đình Chiểu. That is more of a "historical" issue than a "literary" one.

Suppose a student or a writer does not know the circumstances of the birth of the funeral oration or knows but does not feel, love, or appreciate the self-sacrifice of the "Sacrificed Soldiers of Cần Giuộc." In that case, he will definitely "criticize" it. The essay does not reveal the beauty of the work. The following is Nguyễn Đình Chiểu's Tribute to the Sacrificed Fighters of Cần Giuộc:

Oration to the Sacrificed Fighters of Cần Giuộc

Oh my!
The enemy's guns strike our land; The sky knows our people's hearts.
After ten years of hard work, you may not still have a famous reputation. Even though it was lost, an insurgent battle against the French echoed like a gong.
Let us remember the ancient fighters:
Hard-working for a living, thinking about poverty.

Nguyễn đình Chiểu, *author of the poem "Sacrificed Soldiers of Cần Giuộc."*

I am unfamiliar with arrows and horses, need somewhere to go to a training school, only know buffalo fields, and live in the village. Hoeing, plowing, harrowing, planting, hands are used to doing; practicing shields, guns, spears, flags, the eyes have never seen.

The sound of wind and cranes has been fluttering for more than ten months, looking for news like a drought, looking for rain. The flavor of the devotion has been floating around for three years, and they hated villains like the farmers hated grass.

One day, seeing the white shambles covering, we wanted to eat liver. The next day, witnessing the black running chimney, we wanted to go out and bite some neck.

How can anyone come in to cut snakes or chase deer in a massive homeland? The dazzling sun and moon are unsuitable for scoundrels who

hang goats and sell dogs.
Let's wait for someone to demand it, someone to capture it; please try your best to break it off this time. Stay upright; we will get the tigers by hand on this trip.

Quite pitiful:
Initially, they were not strategists nor guards following in the line of marching soldiers; they were just villagers, neighbors, and loyal soldiers who became recruited soldiers. Their bravery knew no bounds.
Eighteen kinds of martial arts – don't long for the training; ninety military battles – don't wait for the disposition.
Outside the kidney, a cloth is not waiting to carry modern arms. They hold a bamboo tree and do not care about a long knife and thick hat.

The old rifle arquebus, fired with a straw wisp, could burn down that religious teaching house. The swords they wore had a machete blade that could cut off the mandarin's head.
Only with the commander's effort, beating the urging drums, did they kick the fences and rush forward, watching the enemies as if they were nothing. No one was afraid of the French shooting small or big bullets, rushing in through the door, risking their lives as if they were nothing.
Those who stabbed sideways, others slashed backward, would shock the black evil spirits.

Some ran first, the others yelled later, never mind the tin ship, the bronze ship, or the guns exploding. Their resilience was truly admirable.

Oh!
These words of gratitude last a long time; they didn't know that the mortal body quickly left. A dream on the battlefield due to the word virtue; they didn't realize the horse skin covering the body. Hundreds of years of hell are the words coming home. Don't wait for the tiger sword to hang on the grave.
Several miles of grass and trees stretch sadly across the Cần GiuộcRiver;
Looking at Trường Binh market, young and older people have two rows of falling tears. It's not that sentence of robbers and fraud cases, but soldiers be willing to fight the enemy, which did not hold the citadel or keep the ramparts, but was adequate to follow the order of the army. But keep on thinking:
Every inch of land, thanks to the Master, is a source of wealth for our country. The bowls of rice and clothes in this land,
 what does it matter to their ancestors? Because of whom, the military officials and soldiers suffer hard, eat snow, and lie in frost? Because of whom was the stronghold smashed and destroyed by rain and wind?
What's the point of living according to the leftist army? They were throwing incense and buckets, overturning the shrines, and seeing that made us

even sadder. What's the point of living as foreign soldiers, sharing light wine and munching on bread? It sounds even more shameful.
It is better to die to get the words downright, and to return to our ancestors is also an honor. Better yet, having to surrender to the French and living with the barbarians is very miserable.

Oh, please stop it!
Pagoda Tông Thạnh is cold in the winter. The red heart sends back the shadow of the full moon. Corner the French for a moment to pay back the anger and regret, his fate drifting with the flowing water.
In such pain, the old mother sat crying for her child, and the late-night light flickered in the tent. Sadly, the weak wife ran to find her husband, and the shadow of a car lingered in front of the alley.

Oh!
A burst of smoke clears, and thousands of years of courage enlighten.
Let its soldiers station Bến Nghé, who created the dark clouds on all four sides. Our ancestors still have Đồng Nai land. Who can save the young children?
Dead but already repaying the debt to the country, their good names are praised all aloud in the Six Provinces. They are now worshiped

> *in the temples, with a reputation that will last forever, and everyone will pay homage to it. Alive to fight the enemy, and dead also fight the enemy. Their souls follow to help the army, forever vowing to take revenge. Live to worship the King; dead also worship the King. The teachings are clear, and a warm word is enough to pay for the merits.*
>
> *The hero's tears could not be wiped dry, pitying the two words "celestial people." The martyr's incense stick was lit to add fragrance, and the gratitude was filled with a sentence of King's earth.*
>
> *Oh, my love and respect!*
> *If being sacred, please accept.*

"Is it true that our studies make it impossible for our people to know the history of our country?" Senior Trần Trọng Kim wrote in the preface to the book "Việt Nam History" nearly a century ago.

Understanding the "country's history" is essential, and the *Lecture Elementary Course* seems valuable because of this.

12. LOVE OTHERS AS LOVING YOURSELF

When you see people in need, feel sorry for them. Seeing disabled people, let's look after them even more.

Seeing the old and weak,
The medicine helps; rice porridge helps.
Heaven does not spare the benevolent,
A person who has virtue will be filled with glory.
(Family's Teaching Song)

That is a poem by Nguyễn Trãi, taught to elementary students in the Lecture Elementary Course.

Nguyễn Trãi (1380-1442) is a famous mandarin; his life is associated with several historical events in our country in ancient times through stories.

There is the story of "Nguyễn Trãi at Nam Quan Pass," then Nguyễn Trãi and "Bình Ngô Đại Cáo," as an independence epic, a declaration after ten years of resistance to the Ming invaders, and finally "the case of Nguyễn Trãi - Thị Lộ."

The poem *"Love others as loving yourself"* is a beautiful moral education lesson. It is as gentle as a mother's lullaby to her child but has a lasting effect. Perhaps there is no need to explain or say anything more, but anyone who reads it, of any age, can feel it.

Today, we understand "tribulation" as calamity, disaster, misfortune, and physical and mental suffering. Therefore, students of the past learned good nature from a young age, knowing how to love the disabled, the hungry, the thirsty, and, in general, people in "distress."

I remember when I was a child. When I went to the temple, my grandmother taught me to put money in the blessing box. When I went to the market, my mother taught me to give money to beggars. At summer noon, I saw a passersby resting in front of our gate. My mother brought out a bowl of rainwater for him to drink.

Learning ethics at school, coming home and being taught by grandmothers and mothers to practice gradually, good qualities and good hearts develop in children's minds.

You probably remember when you were a child, going to school in the morning and afternoon every spring along the banks of the French River, looking at the two rows of red umbrellas blooming, shading the entire river.

Or we walk on the embankment shaded by nipa palm leaves, cooling our feet. We chant the poem *"Love others as loving yourself"* and remember to be grateful to someone who gives us shade and red color, fresh from alum flowers.

The alum tree has fruits in all four seasons, but it primarily blooms during Tết, which is the season for making puffed cakes and rice paper in the homeland. The alum flower is as red as peach blossoms in the North. People in the North soak the alum fruit in wine, and the alum tree is called a cinchona tree.

Thinking back to childhood, I don't know when it penetrated our hearts and minds, but we all have compassion for others.

We love the person who made us a raincoat to cover the rain while going to school; we love the rice ball squeezed by our grandmother's or mother's hands are wrapped in an areca palm and given to us to take with us every morning, for consumption.

At that time, mothers made rice balls very elaborately; it was not simple! The rice is just cooked, a little mushy; take it out while it's still steaming hot, scoop it out, and pour it into the cloth to make about two cups. Gather the four corners of the cloth and knead the rice until it's crushed and smooth; no rice grains can be seen. Then grab four pieces of fabric and twist it around to squeeze the rice tightly until you can't twist it anymore. Open the towel, and squeeze out the round, hard rice with a pointed knob on top, imprinting the folded lines of the towel.

Squeezed rice is delicious and filling. It is sometimes eaten with salted fried shrimp, dried braised fish, or sugar. Now, talking about squeezed rice (in the North, it's called rice balls), I miss the Vietnamese mothers who stay up late and get up early, working hard to prepare meals for their children with endless love.

Back then, when I went to school early, in the morning when it rained, my mother put on my child a long, long covering coat (*áo tơi*) and took me to the other side of the river. That *áo tơi* my mother wore daily to go to the fields and do business in the rainy season was woven from nipa palm leaves (*lá dừa nước*), which was trendy in the past.

For our elementary students, covering coats and rice ball packages are not just something to cover the rain or food to ease hunger; they belong to the soul and the love that a mother sends along with the child on the way to school. Does it come from the elementary lessons of compassion for others in Elementary Course? Even though you now eat so many delicious dishes and wear expensive, gorgeous clothes, they are not better than the rice balls and the covering coat your mother gave you in the past.

> *Heaven does not disregard the benevolent ones*
> *People with great virtues are full of glory.*

Our grandparents and parents believed that It is not a religion or any lofty philosophy but the morality of human life, the morality that created our Vietnamese people in the past.

- *Having the virtue, you can eat whatever you want.*
- *Living kindly, you will undoubtedly meet luck.*

Our proverbs and folk songs are both folk and scholarly, containing a life philosophy vaguely covering all people.

Turning back the pages of history, we also see that our ancient Kings, generation after generation, continued to create our country with all the mountains and rivers we have today, for which we are silently grateful.

Students learn to love their parents, brothers, and people thanks to studying the Lecture Elementary Course from a young age. That love develops into love for their homeland, love for their ancestors, building their homeland, and being proud of their people. We have 4000 years of civilization.

The boy led a blind old woman across the street
(Drawing in Lecture Elementary Course)

Returning to today's schooling in the United States, we no longer hear the saying, "First learn rituals, second learn literature." American schools do not teach children morality, like the Lecture Elementary Course. Vietnamese mothers no longer squeeze rice for their children to take to school. Many Vietnamese parents are worried and afraid that tomorrow, they will not know what will happen to the young generation of Việt Nam. Don't worry too much. Vietnamese people have a "family tradition," which is the foundation of morality, the beginning of building human emotions and morality.

Like Senior Nguyễn Đình Chiểu, a Confucian who grew up in a time when his homeland was devastated by foreign invaders, he maintained his filial piety to his mother and his loyal heart to the people and the country. The love for his mother developed in him and became the love for his homeland, which he said was to repay the favor "every inch of our land."

Even though he was blind, he voluntarily joined the anti-Western movement with Trương Công Định as an advisor, and after the hero Trương Công Định passed away, he composed 12 poems mourning Trương Công Định that have been cherished until now:

> *In the South, his name is celebrated highly,*
> *His battles of Gò Công are famous.*
> *The bullet traces still damaged in white demons' ships.*

The blade's wind makes Huỳnh's name shine brighter.
The banner of rightfulness God has not yet broken,
The Bình Tây's seal was quickly buried.
That fact makes the hero fall into tears,
He silently whispers three mourning words in his soul.

(First poem)

Think back to the article "*Love others as loving yourself.*" However, it is only a moral lesson that teaches old-time students about compassion; it is a nucleus, a precious good seed to create a good person, being grateful to "every inch of the land and vegetable tops" and thankful to ancestors. The first life lesson for children seems to be nothing more valuable than the lesson of "loving people"; it is not only beneficial to the ancients but is still applicable today.

13. NEAR MUD BUT NOT STINK OF MUD

*In the pond, nothing as beautiful as a lotus,
Green leaves, white flowers, and yellow stamens.
Yellow stamens, white flowers, and green leaves,
Near mud but not stink of mud.*

The above folk song was once used as a memorized lesson for students, and it is printed in the book Lecture Elementary Course for Preparatory Classes.

Residing in the South, particularly in Kiến Phong, Cao Lãnh, Đồng Tháp, and Sa Đéc, one can truly grasp the essence of a lotus pond. These serene bodies of water are adorned with lotuses, sprawling like wild grass, a ubiquitous sight that soothes the soul.

Looking at the lotus pond behind the garden, in front of the communal house, pagoda, and school, with lotus leaves covering the water surface and a few white flowers rising above amid the hot, windless summer noon, we see the result:

In the pond, nothing as beautiful as a lotus,

With its rustic yet elegant beauty, the lotus holds deep cultural significance. In ancient times, it symbolized noble values: the integrity of a gentleman, the sophistication of Vietnamese women, and, above all, the great nobility of the Buddha.

Despite being honest, refined, and noble, the image of the lotus is always close and dear to ordinary Vietnamese people:

Tháp Mười has the most beautiful lotus.

The beauty of a small lotus pond in a backyard is highly valued in the United States. People have successfully domesticated the lotus plant to adapt to the local climate, which involves understanding its needs and providing the conditions for its growth.

Lotus plants live in tropical climates and are tolerant of moisture and water. Returning to Đồng Tháp, reliving the scenery of lotus ponds and lotus fields, I realized that my ancestors were in the wild in the past. Coming here from *Đàng Ngoài* (North Việt Nam) to settle down, they knew how to take advantage of what was available to create food, including the dish made from the lotus plant.

When used to wrap cakes and sticky rice, lotus leaves infuse their unique fragrance into the dish, creating a

Lotus: Near mud but not stink of mud.

magical and indescribable flavor that resonates with our souls. Similarly, when mixed with shrimp, meat, herbs, and spices, lotus roots create a special and unique salad that is praised for its deliciousness. These dishes, now prevalent even in high-end restaurants, are a testament to the distinctive flavor of lotus-based cuisine.

The food of the ancients, the Six Provinces people, speaks of a philosophy of food. That is good to eat: delicious food must first be delicious by itself, not because we praise it as delicious: good to think, as Tản Đà and Vũ Bằng said!

Because of the lotus's unique nature, the Lecture Elementary Course wants to borrow the lesson of the lotus plant to educate little students about the crucial importance of maintaining purity and resilience in all situations, even if we live with bad people. It's a lesson that can protect us from harm and keep our hearts pure and bright.

Remember that in folk songs and proverbs, we also have a saying:

- *Near ink, you'll be black; near light, you'll be bright.*
- *Inside the bulb, it'll be round; inside the tube, it'll be long.*

That means no matter what environment or situation one lives in, people will be affected by that situation. So I see the lesson of the Lecture Elementary Course here: "near the mud but not smelling of mud" is not easy. As parents, we must continually reinforce this lesson to our children, teaching them how to grow up so they always keep their hearts pure and bright in the face of all temptations.

History gives us many lessons, many good and bad examples. Like Mr. Phan Văn Trị, who did not follow the French, Tôn Thọ Tường "would rather lose the father's soul to win the husband's heart" – or refuse the benefits of the Bến Tre coroner like Mr. Đồ Chiểu, unlike the case of Mr. Phạm Quỳnh of the Nam Phong Magazine group, who received money from Louis Marty (chief of the secret police) and Albert Sarraut (Governor of Indochina) to do journalism.

Let's go back a bit to lotus-infused tea in our country. Due to the discovery of the unique fragrance and taste of the lotus flower, the status of lotus culture has been enhanced. Since the advent of lotus tea, teas marinated with *lài* (jasmine), *sói* (Fragrant wolfberry flower), and *ngâu* (Aglaia odorat flower) have been brought down to a low level, becoming popular teas. The tea tree originated in China, so its name is Sinensis, and it was introduced to our country, India, and Europe. Tea is present in people's culinary life as a drink and refreshment.

Let's delve into the rich history of lotus-infused tea in our country. The discovery of the unique aroma and flavor of the lotus flower has not only enhanced the status of lotus culture but also profoundly rooted it in our tea traditions. Other teas like Jasmine and Oolong have gained popularity with the introduction of lotus tea. The tea plants from China were introduced to our country, India, and Europe. Tea has become an integral part of people's culinary life, serving as a refreshing drink.

Let's explore the diverse world of tea. How many types of tea are there?

No matter what type of aroma, no matter what brand, there are generally three types of tea, produced in three ways:

- **Green tea** (*trà xanh*) or light tea *(thanh trà)* is a tea that is processed without fermentation and only dried after being rolled to remove essential oils. Green tea gives the water a green color, aroma, and natural sweetness. Most Vietnamese people drink this type of tea.

- **Black tea** is a type of tea that is entirely fermented. It is a tea for red juice, often found in Chinese drink shops in Việt Nam. Europeans like this type.

- **Oolong tea:** Semi-fermented, this tea has a slightly yellowish liquid, is fragrant, and has an astringent taste. Our country's Oolong tea is often drunk in the morning before eating.

In our country, tea and wine have long been used as offerings and ceremonies, such as weddings and funerals.

Two types of precious tea stand out in the rich tea culture of Việt Nam: Long Tỉnh tea, known for its refreshing green notes, and Thiết Quán Âm, a unique Oolong variety with its distinct aroma and taste.

It's a captivating journey of cultural exchange from China to Việt Nam. As tea traversed from North to South, its consumption evolved, giving rise to unique regional differences in how it's enjoyed.

Tea from the North is not just a beverage; it's a romanticized street trend. The image of a fresh tea shop lady has been immortalized in Bắc Hà literature with its romantic details.

Tea is also prepared and sold on the market streets in Hue, called Huế tea, especially mixed with ginger, but the history of tea vendors in Huế is not as rich as in the North!

In the South, we also drink fresh Huế tea, but no one sells tea at the intersection or in the market. Travelers in Six Provinces drink rainwater, which is free to drink; every house has a pot in the front yard.

Only in the South is there an iced tea that is so special and unique! Indeed, no one knows when iced tea appeared in the South and who had the initiative. However, iced tea appeared after the ice-making industry in our country.

If you've been back to Six Provinces more than once, waiting to cross bridge Bến Lức or ferry Mỹ Thuận in the past, you'll always order a glass of iced tea to quench your thirst. Iced tea traveling on country roads, bus stations, ferry terminals, and coffee shops... is an "iced tea culture."

The old American expeditionary soldiers who entered Sàigòn also had the habit of ordering a glass of "Sàigòn Tea," which was cheap and allowed them to sit and sip for a long time with the ladies in popular cafes. Perhaps that's why, since then, in wine bars in Sàigòn, when American guests offer waitresses a glass of wine, she immediately calls "Sàigòn Tea" a glass of wine. Still, it's just tea. The ladies do not get drunk while serving customers.

The popularity of iced tea transcends borders, making its way to the United States from Việt Nam. It's a common sight in pho shops and Vietnamese restaurants, where American and Mexican diners often opt for a refreshing glass of iced tea after enjoying a bowl of beef noodle *phở*.

It's been a long time since I had the opportunity to recall the memorized lesson "The Lotus Plant" in the Lecture Elementary Course. The four folk songs begin with:

In the pond, nothing can compare to the lotus!

It evokes many memories in us. The countryside's beautiful, poetic, and peaceful images rush into our hearts and minds simultaneously. The image *"Green leaves and white flowers are surrounded by yellow pistil – Yellow pistil and white flowers and green leaves"* is so cute. We felt sorry for the lotus pond behind the house, for our country mothers, or a memory of our own.

Being close to the mud but not smelling of it is the wish of the ancients, expressed in the folk song "Lotus Plant," and it will forever be the wish of us and our future descendants.

The folk song "Lotus Plant" describes the lotus pond scene, the beauty of the lotus, and the nobility of the lotus flower, a lesson that has long been ingrained in the souls of Lecture Elementary Course students. Now that we reread it, we ask ourselves how to live like a lotus flower: "near the mud but not smell of mud."

PART II

FAMILY AND SCHOOL

1. *Go to school on time.*
2. *As a person, you have to go to school.*
3. *What is the purpose of going to school?*
4. *Students are grateful to the teachers.*
5. *Strong Will of a man.*
6. *Must keep a pure heart.*
7. *My homeland is the most beautiful place.*
8. *A delicious meal.*
9. *Grandma lulls her grandchild.*
10. *One Who Goes, One Who Stays.*
11. *Going to the Market to Pay.*
12. *Soggy Rain and Chilly Wind*

Go to school on time
(Drawing in Lecture Elementary Course)

The teacher lectures during class
(Drawing in Lecture Elementary Course)

1. GO TO SCHOOL ON TIME

Xuân is going to school; he looks cheerful.
Meeting young Thu in the middle of the way,
Asking him: Why are you in such a hurry?
The drum is still not playing; why bother going to school?

After half a century, I was still moved when I re-read the Elementary school reading text that every student knew. That reading, in the poem form of two seven-six-eight words: *"Go to school must be on time,"* opened the First-Grade curriculum.

It was not random that the author set the article *"Go to school on time"* at the beginning of the textbook. The meaning of the reading exercise, which taught students to be punctual, has been deeply imprinted on the young generations of Việt Nam in the past, becoming a habit as a form of discipline so they can later become citizens who know how to respect time in all activities.

Indeed, in the past, our country did not have clocks, people measured time: during the day, they looked at the sun; at night, they heard the cocks crowing and birds chirping. Farmers look at the rising and lowering river water to measure time by how many puffs of tobacco roll they smoke or half of a betel bait!

In public places, time is calculated according to the *"canh"* (1 canh= 2 hours) and is announced by the sound of the "canh" drum, so the probability of a difference of two or three hours is expected.

We have heard the saying: Officials are busy, people are late. That's how it has always been.

In the past, students were rarely late for school. Students who are late do not dare to go to school. They must be escorted to class by their parents or siblings. At that time, going to school late, even for a legitimate reason, was embarrassing and awkward to the friends.

My school has three classes and three classrooms. The drum hangs in the Junior Class, at the back of the school. The teacher assigns the oldest student, usually the class leader, to be the drummer. Students at that time lived far from school, in gardens and fields, because only two or three villages had one primary school (Level I). We came to school very early, sometimes two hours, and played around the school and in the market house near the school. Hearing three drum beats means preparing to go back to school. Then, after hearing a drum beat (about 10 minutes), run back to the classroom to line up, listen to 3 drum beats (about 5 minutes), and then go into the school together according to the teacher's instructions.

The traditional drum, a fond memory from my school days, instilled in me the habit of punctuality. Even as I progressed to the province for further studies, the sound of the drum remained my reliable timekeeper. The provincial school, with its gate that opened and closed punctually, ensured I never missed a class due to tardiness.

As I matured, I found myself adapting to the changing times. The traditional drum, once the sole timekeeper of my daily routine, was replaced by a Western rooster clock in my home. This modern timepiece, with its luminous blue hours that glowed beautifully at night, starkly contrasted with the drum. It was a symbol of the cultural shift towards modern timekeeping. In a solemn gesture, my mother placed it in the middle of the altar in front of the incense burner, inviting our neighbors to check the time.

Then, I got my first Cita watch (?) when I entered seventh grade (today's sixth grade). It was always on my hand to remind me to be on time. Xuân and Thu are two elementary school students who answered questions in the reading exercise "Going to school on time." Fifty years ago, they still made many unforgettable impressions on me.

Memories of students were sentimental, like memories of the drum signaling the time to go to school, which are the punctuality lessons that the Lecture Elementary Course taught me since I was a child.

Today, we have many time-measuring and time-telling devices. Clocks, clocks in the car, clocks in the phone, on the radio, on the TV, on the refrigerator, on the microwave... It's in the workplace, the sleeping place, the cleaning place... there are clocks everywhere. Yet we deliberately don't see, hear, care, or feel shy... enough "Four No's" to be late. Dare to be late for a wedding, late for a meeting, late for a concert...

Even though we remember or forget the Lecture Elementary Course, we probably still remember the four verses:

> *Xuân is going to school, he looks cheerful.*
> *Meeting young Thu in the middle of the way,*
> *Asking him: Why are you in such a hurry?*
> *The drum is not playing yet, why bother to go to school?*

It reminds us of the lesson: Be punctual.

2. AS A PERSON YOU HAVE TO GO TO SCHOOL

Nowadays, when children grow up, they are old enough for their parents to send them to school. School is normal and natural, like eating, drinking, and working. There is nothing to discuss; the question is why we have to go to school.

However, the children of the previous generation differed in the old days and at the beginning of the 20th century. Not every Vietnamese family could afford to send their children to school to learn Chinese, French, and National Words. Going to school became a "privilege" for those with money and power!

Again, because some people are uneducated, poor, and doomed, they don't see going to school as a need and a key to opening the door of intelligence, some luggage to enter life. That's why people say:

> *First student, second farmer*
> *Running out of rice, running around*
> *First farmers, second students!*

Or

> *The son of a mandarin is destined to become an official*
> *The little monks at the temple sweep banyan leaves...*

Hence, in the Lecture Elementary Course, the Preparatory book (Grade Two), the authors have the lesson "*As A Person You Have To Go To School*" and begins with two aphorisms:

> "*That jade is neither filed nor polished,*
> *It will become useless and wasted jade.*"

That's right!

Without someone digging for it, filing, polishing, and producing it, Jade will forever remain just a stone lying dormant deep in the ground. Gold that is not dug up, filtered, and refined is useless. Reading those two sentences, our childhood students immediately understood and were "enlightened": why we must go to school.

The author of the Elementary Course continued:

> "*Human beings are no different*
> *Studying is precious, and foolish is ruining the life.*"

Before the French invasion, our grandparents learned Chinese and the old Vietnamese character "Nôm." At

Father teaches his son: "That jade is neither filed nor polished / It will become useless and wasted jade." So, "As A Person You Have To Go To School"
(Drawing in Lecture Elementary Course)

that time, they mainly learned how to be human beings and gentlemen. Our ancestors adapted from Chinese that way of learning.

The Chinese basic books were the Four Books and the Five Classics[1]. People learning Confucianism must know how to preserve the Three Relationships and the Five Virtues[2]. Thanks to that learning, the feudal regime was stable and developed for a long time, like Vietnamese history.

---

1 *Four Books*: Great Learning, Middle Ages, Analects, Mencius.
   Five Classics (Scriptures): Poetry, Letters, Transmutation, Rites, and Spring – Autumn.
2 *Three Relationship*: King-subject, father-son, husband-wife.
   Five Virtues: Humanism-Righteousness-Ceremony-Wisdom-Loyalty.

Our Kings and lords in the past knew how to choose talented people to help the country through examinations.

The lesson *"being a person, you have to go to school"* in the book Lecture Elementary Course refers to learning the national and Western languages.

When the French occupied the Southern region, they established the Thông Ngôn school (for Interpreters) and the Tham Mưu training school (the Commander) and then opened the Primary School, which we used to call the Village School.

Please remember that in the beginning, in many places in Six Provinces, the village school was located in Village Communal House (Đình Làng). When did our country's communal houses exist? According to Mr. Ngô Sĩ Liên in *"Đại Việt Sử Ký Toàn Thư"* (Đại Việt Complete History Collection) our Communal House dates back to 1242 during the Trần Dynasty.

That year, Mr. Trần Thủ Độ took the initiative to introduce a policy of "close to the people, close to the people," so he organized the basic administrative units of the village and built a public road called the Communal House, appointing a Chief to look after it. He considered and provided public fields to cover the village communal house's affairs.

Meanwhile, the Chinese Communal House was built on the official road to serve as a post station and a service place for military officials on their way to work. There are two types of communal houses on the main roads:

- *Đoãn Đình*: Near communal house: The communal house was built 5 miles apart.

- *Trường Đình*: Far communal houses were built 10 miles apart.

(Reading the Chinese story "Chu-Han contention"- (*Hán Sở Tranh Hùng*) we all praise the "good" spirit; when Xiang Yu (Hạng Võ)'s superior was besieged at Cai Ha, he beheaded himself to hand over to Đình Trưởng, who was the ferryman and also the chief of the communal house in Cai Ha area.

Meanwhile, in Việt Nam, in the Six Provinces region, almost every village had a communal house built by the people and asked the King to confer it for worship. Vietnamese communal houses both worship gods and center local community cultural activities. They have a self-governing system: "village and commune autonomy," so the folk saying:

The King's order lost to the village charter.

In the South, communal houses are often built according to the character Cong, or upside-down Dinh, facing south, away from residential areas to avoid noise and pollution and to show respect to the gods.

The communal house in Six Provinces has three separate areas: Trong communal house, dedicated to worshiping gods, is only open on worship days, and only Mr. Tu comes in every night to burn incense; the Frontal Communal House, where folk worship is held; the Central Communal House in the middle is for officials to worship and party. On both sides of the Central Communal House are two corridors on the right and left for villagers to celebrate.

We are familiar with the village communal house, and the generation is over 60 years old. Every year, the "Kỳ Yên" festival attracts many villagers, young men and women.

Passing by the Đình, I removed my hat to greet it,

No matter how many tiles it has, I love you that much.

The village communal house has many tiles because it is roofed in two layers: the lower layer is painted and called "mat tile," and the upper layer is called "rich tile" to resist rain and storms and last a long time.

The pillars are massive, round, and polished. So in the countryside, if something is significant, people say:

Big as a pillar of Đình

Or:

The pillar is so big that one person can't hug it all.

In conclusion, the author of the Elementary Course wrote:

"Those 'jackfruit' guys are so special
Who still bribes and invites them?"

The author criticizes ignorant people for encouraging students to try their best to go to school.

"Thick jackfruit" means ignorant, not knowing anything. I don't know who thinks that "thick jackfruit" means childish or that the writing "not full is jackfruit" is ignorant.

When reading the Lecture Elementary Course and discussing learning the National Language, we remember the Governor General of Indochina Merlin[3]. In 1924, he abandoned the Confucian education system and replaced it with the national language learning style. He established the primary education system, which taught the national language. From there, the New Learners school began, and those who followed the French criticized the Old Learners school. Some people used their education in the New Hoc faction to fight against the French.

As the Lecture Elementary Course taught students in the past, educated people are as precious as gems and always respected by everyone.

Throughout history, intellectuals have been the bedrock of our society, their knowledge and wisdom guiding our nation's progress. From the traditional 'scholars' to the modern-day intellectuals, their contributions have always been invaluable, helping to shape our country and its people.

---

3 Governor General of Indochina Merlin was bombed and killed by Phạm Hồng Thái in Sa Điện, Guangzhou, China, on June 18, 1924, but luckily escaped death. Phạm Hồng Thái's real name is Phạm Thành Tích (1896-1924), a patriotic young man who fought against the French and joined the revolutionary organization "Tân Tân Xã." His grave is currently in Hoàng Hoa Cương Guangzhou, along with 72 Chinese martyrs.

In their bid to create a class of followers, the French inadvertently ignited the spark of their own opposition. Vietnamese intellectuals and the newly educated youth, in a display of remarkable resilience, rose up against the French, challenging their rule and asserting their intellectual prowess. This act of defiance, rooted in the intellectual strength of our people, played a significant role in shaping our nation's history.

Education is not just a part of our culture but a significant force that shapes it. Our people value and promote not only the educated but also the learning process itself. This cultural emphasis on education has fostered a tradition of studiousness among Vietnamese youth. Whether it's the study of Confucian, Western, or American languages, our people consistently demonstrate their intelligence, diligence, and ability to achieve high rankings. This is a testament to our value of education, which is not just a part of our culture, but a force that deeply ingrains in our family and clan lifestyle, and something we can all be proud of.

3. WHAT IS THE PURPOSE OF GOING TO SCHOOL?

Before the French occupation, our education system was rooted in the learning of Chinese characters, a testament to our resilience and adaptability. Despite our country's dependence on China and the spread of their national language to us, we maintained our unique identity. Even after independence, we continued to use Chinese characters and had an examination system to select talented individuals. The Chinese characters used in our country were the same as those in China, but our pronunciation was distinct, a symbol of our cultural independence.

Our country's education system, in the past, was a shining example of fairness and equality. Organized examinations ensured that students were not differentiated by social class. The *Quốc Tử Giám* (National Children School), established by the King, was the only exception, providing separate education for the King's descendants and the children of mandarins. This commitment to equality in education is an inspiration for us today.

When the French occupied our country, it first turned the Southern region into a colony. Then, France used the National Language script to replace Chinese characters and built a new education system.

The article 'What is the purpose of going to school?' Lecture Elementary Course for Preparatory classes (*Cours Préparatoire*) sheds light on learning the National Language during the French rule of our country. It vividly illustrates the purpose of teaching and learning *Quốc Ngữ*: The primary goal of education was to equip students to read and write poetry. At that time, the village lacked individuals who could read the national language or interpret the poems from the documents. The secondary aim of education was to enable students to read newspapers and imitate their style.

At that time, the Southern region had Gia Định Báo[4], the first national-language newspaper to propagate French colonial policies.

---

4 The French government published Gia Định Báo newspaper in Sàigòn in 1865. In the northern region, Dai Nam Dong Van Nhut Bao, written in Nho (Chinese) script, was born in 1892. It was not until 1907 that the national language section was added by Mr. Nguyễn Van Vinh, editor, and Phan Ke Binh, secretary.

In August 1868, the French assigned Mr. Trương Vĩnh Ký[52] to oversee the work (editor) along with Mr. Tôn Thọ Tường, Huỳnh Tịnh Của, and Trương Minh Ký. The first newspaper in our country was state-owned; the writers (journalists) worked for the French government.

Education under the French rule was not just about learning, it was about progress. The introduction of scientific subjects that were previously absent in our traditional education system was a significant leap forward. The Lecture Elementary Course, which taught morality, filial piety, and respect for French government laws, aimed to shape citizens into honest people.

It is true that which political regime created that educational policy to train people to serve the regime, or at least not to oppose that government!! Let's delve into the historical context. In the past, during feudal times, our education system was deeply influenced by Chinese education. Its aim was to train gentlemen based on the Four Letters and Five Classics, thereby preserving a social system and hierarchy of Kings and soldiers. This system was deeply ingrained in the people, bound by

---

5 Trương Vĩnh Ký (1837-1898), a native of Cái Mơn, Vĩnh Long in the Southern region, played a pivotal role in the Gia Định Bao newspaper. At the age of 4, he was sent abroad by a French missionary to study religion. In 1863, he was dispatched by France to serve as an interpreter for Phan Thanh Giản's embassy to France, advocating for the redemption of the three provinces of Biên Hòa, Gia Định, and Định Tường. In 1869, the French entrusted him with the role of overseeing the articles (Editor) of Gia Định Bo newspaper, a position he held until his death on September 1, 1898, at the age of 61.

the concept of legitimacy, a concept that China is now reviving with the restoration of Confucius.

The French came in to overthrow the old value system, abolish the King's absolute power, eliminate the middle class of mandarins and scholars, and replace it with a new value system, a new education system, and new information through the national language. Lecture Elementary Course contributes to building that value system. French education does not teach students to become patriotic citizens. Still, it wants to create a class of enforcers and intermediaries to rule over their people, and to some extent, this intermediary class is the modern, Western-educated class; they are also proud of the majority of their poor, uneducated compatriots!

Reread the article "What is the purpose of going to school?" We understand the French plot to eliminate Chinese characters and use the National language in education to create a new class of Western learners. Thus, the patriotic scholars, such as Mr. Nguyễn Đình Chiểu, Phan Văn Trị, etc., boycotted the national language.

The author of Lecture Elementary Course talks about the purpose of learning as follows:

The author, in a unique and personal reflection, shares the purpose of their learning journey. They express,

> *'You asked me why I went to school. I am sharing with you my unique perspective. I went to school to learn how to decipher the letters people sent me and compose the letters I sent to others. I*

went to school to learn how to read books and the Daily newspaper; I would emulate it if I found something inspiring. I went to school to learn how to calculate, to gain knowledge, and to understand the importance of hygiene for a healthy body.'

But the main thing I go to school for is to know morality, to understand how to behave like a filial son and an honest person."

The lesson "What's the purpose of going to school?" reminds me of when I was little, no one told me what to go to school for. Later, when I took my child to school on the first day, I did not teach him why he had to go to school! People only say how to learn how to be good at Math, Literature, Biology, and how to get into university.

I went to school to learn how to decipher the letters people sent me and compose the letters I sent to others.
(Drawing in Lecture Elementary Course)

Yet, since the last century, Lecture Elementary Course teachers have known how to introduce elementary classes to teach students what they go to school for. Few Lecture Elementary Course students remember the reading exercise "What is the purpose of going to school?"

Half a century later, as we revisit these words, we are reminded of the author's poignant description of the benefits of education. It's a bittersweet journey down memory lane, recalling the long series of childhood, the lessons of the Lecture Elementary Course, and the joy of flipping through its pages to see who could find the most pictures.

The summary of the lesson "What is the purpose of going to school," Lecture Elementary Course stated that:

People who do not study do not know the reason.
(Nhân bất học, bất tri lý)

It's a valid point. Uneducated people often need more reason! The words **Learning** and **Reason** here at the Lecture Elementary Course are so advanced that they surpass the standard curriculum.

Written for parents on the occasion of the 2004 school opening season

4. STUDENTS ARE GRATEFUL TO TEACHERS

This article tells the story of a French mandarin named Carnot in the ancient France who returned to visit to his homeland in his free time. When he passed by the school in the village, he saw the teacher who taught him as a child, now with gray hair, sitting in class. He then came to visit...

When I was a child, students of our age often talked about Mr. Carnot. It became common knowledge; everyone knew him. Now again, we still remember printing the picture Mr. Carnot drew in the Elementary Course Lecture Book: The image of the French mandarin dressed majestically, wearing high boots, bowing to greet the teacher... once inspired a sense of pride. His will do, Mr. Carnot. Childhood psychology at a young age combines wanting to be an official and the spirit of Eastern morality and Respect for teachers.

The spirit of respecting teachers is everywhere. Although perhaps in the East, that spirit is more profound, expressing the Eastern Doctrine.

In the treasury of Vietnamese and Chinese literature and folklore, there are many examples of students being grateful to their teachers and many beautiful stories, much nobler than Mr. Carnot. Some Elementary Course Lecturers spread the story of Mr. Carnot to praise the "great French," while our Kings and officials consider them "White Demons!!

Mr. Carnot greeted the teacher
(Lecture Elementary Course)

In our country, we have not only been grateful to our Teachers but also Respect (that is too much in the French and the American). The Asian family and society are grateful and respect the teacher. The Teacher is ranked only after the King in the hierarchy of King-Teacher-Father. Many Kings respected and were thankful to their

Teachers, even the Kings. Please listen to what people say about Teacher (on the New Year days):

> *The first day at my father's house*
> *On the second day at the wife's house,*
> *On the third day, go to the teacher's house.*

During the three important days at the beginning of the year, Tết, students spend the third day visiting their Teachers.

I remember when I was young, in third grade at the village school, on Tết, my mother prepared a dozen first-batch eggs[6], a tea bag, and two sticky rice Tết cakes to make present to my teacher. (At the end of third grade, I took the Middle Course[7] entrance exam in Gò Công province and passed fourth place, so I got a scholarship and could continue studying).

Remember the sentence:

> *- Want to go cross the river, build a bridge*
> *- Want the children be literary, respect the teacher.*

Or:

> *- In all vocations, the one of a teacher is the most precious.*

---

6 *The first-batch eggs:* of a hen is laid by a hen for the first time, very scarce. Folklore believes that chicken seeds are more nutritious than regular seeds, meaning chicken seeds after the first generation.

7 *Middle Course (Fr: Cours Moyen):* In a significant development in 1912, Mr. Phạm Quỳnh proposed a national language program for elementary school levels (fifth, fourth, and third grades). This program, upon completion, allows students to pass the Basic exam and progress to second grade, where they continue their studies for 2 years.

All of them express the Vietnamese's love for their teachers.

In the Southern region during the early Nguyễn Dynasty, in the 17th century, there was Mr. Võ Trường Toản, a hermit, a master who trained for Gia Long many famous mandarins, such as Trịnh Hoài Đức, Lê Quang Định, Ngô Nhân Tịnh...

He passed away in 1792, his disciples buried him in Hòa Hưng, Gia Định. After the French occupied the East (Biên Hòa, Gia Định, Định Tường), Tự Đức ordered him to be reburied and brought him back to bury in village Bảo Thạnh, Ba Tri (Bến Tre) in 1865. So, clearly, King Tự Đức also knew that gratitude and respect for the teacher were no less than that of Tử Cống in China.

We heard Mr. Carnot say to his students after entering the classroom to greet the teacher:

> *"I was able to survive, especially thanks to my parents, and then to my teacher, and thanks to my teacher's hard work in teaching me, I made the career I have today."*

Our country's teachers teach literacy, morality, and ethics so that students become honest people.

In Literature and Ceremony, in ancient schools, Ceremony is still the top priority:

> *First is Rites, Second is Literature.*

That was the philosophy of our ancient education system and remained until April 30, 1975.

Part II
• FAMILY AND SCHOOL 159

A student on the way met his teacher. He stop and crossed his arms to greet him.
(Drawing in Lecture Elementary Course)

When I entered the Pedagogical University in the 1960s, the spirit of *"First Learning Rites, Later Learning Literature"* was still strong among us. Although the manners and respect shown are different from the past, students in my generation of teachers still cherish their teachers even though they are young like us. During Tết, my house was crowded with students, so I had to stay home throughout the third day to celebrate Spring with them. Oh, how noble!

Without the teacher, you cannot make it!

The aphorism sums up the role of a teacher of one's country.

Returning to Mr. Carnot's story in the Lecture Elementary Course, just one aspect is gratitude to the Teacher. That is the French concept. In America, even gratitude fades in the view of students, families, and American society towards the Teacher. That concept is expressed in names such as:

- School District
- School Area

Instead of like our country:

- Education Department
- Department of Education

The story Mr. Carnot told in the Lecture Elementary Course, now rereading it after decades still seems like it was just yesterday! Fast-forward half a century.

The students of our Lecture Elementary Course generation who are lost here don't know if they still have enough minds to remember the old days and old stories. Anyway, on the first day of school, recalling the story of Mr. Carnot, the story of *"**Before: Learning Rites; After: Learning Literature**,"* is not useless.

Written on the opening day of school in 2004.

5. STRONG WILL OF A MAN

When we were in high school, our teacher taught us a lot about being boys during Vietnamese Literature class. At that time, our souls felt excited, optimistic, and proud, and everyone was eager to study and succeed so that they could have the opportunity to serve the country.

For young students eight years old in the second grade of elementary school, Lecture Elementary Course has given the song "Strong Will of a Man" in the form of a folk song, memorizing it so that students can practice reading, which is very meaningful:

> *"Be a man determined to cultivate himself,*
> *Don't worry about your career; don't worry about debt.*
> *When you become good, God will help you.*
> *Be a man, thinking five (times) caring seven (times), makes you proud."*

Growing up, we can forget everything our teachers taught us about Philosophy, History, Algebra, Geometry... but not the folk songs and memorized lessons. It has penetrated our hearts and become something that belongs to us.

The old way of learning started teaching people about *"self-cultivation"* and morality before teaching about other specialized areas. That's why we say:

Before: Learning ritual; after: Learning literature

Now, people call education creating an "Eastern value" different from the "Western value" that humanity follows.

People in the past studied Confucianism, the teachings of saints and sages. They cared about cultivating themselves before thinking about making a name to take charge of the country's affairs later. Even though I learned Chinese, I always had to fight against China to gain independence, so I still feel grateful to Confucius, like our ancestors who established the **Temple of Literature** (**Văn Miếu**), Thăng Long, in 1070, under the Lý Dynasty, now it's still **Văn Miếu, the Temple of Literature** in Hà Nội.

So, in the South, where the land has just been discovered, do we have a temple of literature?

Going back to the history of the formation of the Southern land a bit: In 1698, Le Thanh Marquis Nguyễn Hữu Cảnh obeyed Lord Nguyễn Phước Chu's order to establish an administrative foundation in Đàng Trong, establishing Trấn Biên (Biên Hòa) and Phiên Trấn (Gia Định), establishing Vietnamese sovereignty in this place. Seventeen years later, the Trấn Biên Temple of Literature was established in Tấn Lai village, Phước Vinh district, now Bửu Long ward, Biên Hòa. Unlike its counterpart in Thăng Long, this temple holds a special place in the hearts of the Đồng Nai people, as it symbolizes their deep respect and honor for Confucius, the founder of Confucianism.

Văn Miếu, the Temple of Literature, Thăng Long, in 1070
(Drawing in Lecture Elementary Course)

The '*Đại Nam nhất thống chí*' (Geographical record of Việt Nam), published in 1882, describes the Temple of Literature in Trấn Biên (Văn Thánh Trấn Biên) as a place of breathtaking beauty:

It is nestled amidst beautiful mountains and rivers, adorned with lush vegetation. The interior *is a sight to behold, with exquisitely carved pillars and an abundance of bananas tree and sapodillas tree, their large fruits a testament to the fertility of the land.*

Văn Thánh Trấn Biên was once the cradle of Đồng Nai's culture, producing erudite scholars who loved their homeland, such as Võ Trường Toản, Trịnh Hoài Đức, Ngô Nhơn Tịnh, Lê Quang Định, Nguyễn Đình Chiểu, Phạm Đăng Hưng...

When the French occupied Sàigòn (1859) and Biên Hòa (1861), they burned Văn Thánh Trấn Biên, of which we no longer see any traces. From 1945 to 1975, no one heard anything about it, and no one thought of restoring the Trấn Biên Temple of Literature!

Lecture Elementary Course writes the last four verses of the folk song to memorize:

"Heaven gives birth, Heaven won't abandon,
At Wind and Clouds Assembly, the heroes will take action.
Wisdom is inside the heart,
Has iron grinding makes perfect needle one day."

Upon closer examination, the Lecture Elementary Course delves into the concept of 'Heaven's Way' ("*Đạo Trời*"). In the realm of Confucianism, this encompasses 'The Way of Man' and 'The Way of Heaven'. 'Heaven's Way' refers to the cosmic order, the reason behind the existence of Heaven and Earth, and the act of creation, often referred to as the 'Creator' ("*Con Tạo*").

The ancients believed that if people knew how to cultivate themselves, heaven would help them, and one day, they would meet *"festival of the wind and clouds."* (*"hội phong vân"*) That's why the folk song has the sentence, "*The wind and clouds meet the heroes and take action.*"

Why do we say, "*Your mind is falling in your stomach*"?

My grandparents used to say: *The stomach makes the stomach bears* or use the word "dull stomach" (*tối dạ*) to mean slow, unintelligent, and "bright stomach" (*sáng dạ*) to tell intelligent, quick to understand.

People often say:
Having a big head is foolish
Having a big d... is wise.

The stark contrast in how Eastern and Western cultures perceive intelligence is an intriguing observation with profound societal implications. In the East, we believe that human intelligence is contained in the lower part of the body – the solar plexus. This belief directly opposes the French view that wisdom is stored in the head, particularly the brain, and shapes our understanding of intelligence and its role in our lives. These contrasting views are a testament to the rich diversity of human thought and culture. They are a powerful reminder of the importance of respecting and understanding different perspectives, enlightening and broadening our minds.

Saying, *"Strong Will of a man,"* did the ancients underestimate women and heroines?

It's important to acknowledge the societal progress we've made in redefining gender roles. In the past, our society had a clear division of roles and responsibilities between men and women, both in the family and society. However, we've come a long way. Vietnamese women are now respected in different positions, and we take pride in being ahead of many other countries worldwide. This progress is a source of inspiration and pride for us all.

Recently, it was said that Biên Hòa had rebuilt Văn Thánh Miếu Trấn Biên to celebrate the 300th anniversary of Biên Hòa's founding.

Hopefully, the end of heaven and earth will gather in Đồng Nai, Gia Định. This land has a gentle climate, simple people, and fertile land, with long rivers and vast seas; it is truly a spiritual and outstanding land that heaven has reserved for the Hồng Lạc grandchildren. *(Thái Văn Kiểm, The Noble Beauties, 1957)*

Then our children and grandchildren sing loudly:
Nhà Bè's water flow is divided into two
Anyone who returns to Gia Định, Đồng Nai,
keeps returning.

Regardless of your destination, Gia Định or Đồng Nai, your journey will inevitably lead you to this International Junction. It is a testament to when our forefathers traversed these lands, laying the foundation for the **Pearl of the Far East – Sàigòn.**

Let's delve into the history of Vĩnh Long's Temple of Literature.

When was this esteemed institution first established, and what events led to its formation?

- Remember, after losing 3 Eastern provinces, King Tự Đức was in pain because there were the graves of Mr. and Mrs. Phạm Đăng Hưng, the King's grandparents. Tự Đức, under pressure from the French, ordered the disbandment of Trương Công Định's insurgent army in exchange for the King's grandfather's tomb not being destroyed.

In 1864, Tự Đức ordered Phan Thanh Giản to build the Temple of Literature Vĩnh Long and the Testing Institution An Giang (Châu Đốc) to replace the Temple of Literature Trấn Biên and National Test Institution Gia Định, which the French destroyed.

Temple of Literature Vĩnh Long is on the road from Vĩnh Long to Trà Vinh, completed in 1867. It is a place to worship Confucius and 72 saints, later worshiping Phan Thanh Giản and Đốc Học Nguyễn Thông.

Before 1975, this road was named **Văn Thánh**. It was also the birthplace of many talented descendants of the 'Vãng country,' a term used to refer to the prosperous southern region of Việt Nam and the South Việt Nam.

1867, France took control of Vĩnh Long on June 20 of the lunar calendar. Despite this, the people's spirit remained unbroken. On July 5, 1867, Mr. Phan Thanh Giản, a symbol of this resilience and a prominent figure in the resistance against the French, chose to end his life. However, the French did not order the destruction of *Văn Thánh Miếu Vĩnh Long*, as they had done in Trấn Biên.

Following the French occupation of Vĩnh Long, the management of *Văn Thánh Miếu* was entrusted to the local Minh Hương people. During King Thành Thái's reign in 1889, it was handed over to Long Hồ village for management. The Vĩnh Long Temple, a proud testament to our rich cultural and religious heritage, is maintained and worshiped with reverence twice a year in the second and eighth months of the lunar calendar.

In chronological order, our country has 4 Temples of Literature: **Thăng Long, Trấn Biên** (rebuilt), **Huế**, and **Vĩnh Long**. As for Testing Institution Gia Định and Testing Institution Châu Đốc, no traces are left, which is unfortunate.

The lesson "Strong Will of a Man" in the Lecture Elementary Course has been passed for nearly a century, but repeating it to today's generation is still not without its benefits.

Although ancient learning and examinations were different from today, they were of paramount importance and aimed at training talented people and intellectuals for the country. The path to a career or finding an opportunity to compete to become a man must go through the 'official' alley, a tradition that commands deep respect even today.

Throughout history, Confucianism has been a guiding force in Vietnamese society, emphasizing morality and self-cultivation. This philosophy has shaped our nation, fostering a culture of sacrifice and producing a wealth of scholars dedicated to noble causes.

Reflecting on the 50s and 60s, one must recognize the figure of Nguyễn Công Trứ, a Confucian writer and poet with a strong sense of self-determination. He served as a minister during the reigns of Minh Mạng and Thiệu Trị. He hails from Hà Tĩnh and was born to Nguyễn Công Tấn, who held the position of Marquis during the Lê Mạt dynasty. His life and work are a testament to the enduring influence of Confucianism in Việt Nam.

When King Gia Long finished eliminating the Lê Dynasty-Trịnh Lord-Mạc Dynasty in Bắc Hà, he traveled to the North. Then, Nguyễn Công Trứ came to present the peaceful hearing "Thái Bình Tập Sách," which the King praised, but the King did not use it!

He was determined to pass the Baccalaureate (1813) and then the doctorate in Hà Nội (1819) and was hired by Minh Mạng. He successively held positions: Commissioner of Sử Quán (1820), District Head Hải Dương, Advisor of canton Thanh Hóa...

He was sent many times to defeat the enemy from North to South. There was a time when he and Trương Minh Giảng defended Trấn Tây, who became Tuần Vũ An Giang. What's unique about Nguyễn Công Trứ is that his poetry has a heroic spirit, urging people to take on the responsibility of the mountains and rivers, compete passionately, and go beyond that time's usual poetic style.

Re-read his poem "Strong Will of a Man" and review the development of the literature and culture of our ancestors through the formation of the Temple of Literature from Thăng Long to Vĩnh Long to see that the ancient learning of my ancestors is genuinely authentic.

Senior Nguyễn Công Trứ's life is a testament to his unwavering character. He defied the political boundaries of his family, spanning the Lê Dynasty and the Nguyễn Dynasty, to serve his homeland, settle his debts, and fulfill his personal aspirations.

These days, thinking and doing mirroring the principles of Mr. Nguyễn Công Trứ are not easy. His approach to work has become a guiding light for our people.

The lesson from the Lecture Elementary Course continues to hold immense value for us. Its teachings have not only enriched our understanding but also guided our personal growth.

6. MUST KEEP YOUR HEART PURE

There was a lesson on memorizing for the students, the folk song: "The Stork Goes Out to Eat at Night":

"The stork comes out to eat at night
It landed on a soft branch and flipped its neck into the pond.
Sir, please save me!
If I have an evil heart, you can cook with bamboo shoots.
If you cook, please cook with clear water
Don't stir up turbid water, that hurt the little stork's heart."

(Lecture Elementary Course)

Lessons memorized, but "in childhood," "two days at school"... our students keep repeating the piece because this folk song is easy to learn and remember. Fifty years later, reading this article seems like just yesterday, with my horseshoe haircut,[8] carrying my schoolbag to the village school, over 5 kilometers away.

At our age, having the "three words" in our hearts, reading the stories of *Phạm Công Cúc Hoa, Thạch Sanh Killed the Ogle*, or writing a form asking for permission from the village to celebrate a death anniversary[9] is more precious than gold.

Each lesson in the Lecture Elementary Course set illustrates the lesson content. The pictures in the book are drawn squarely and printed in wood carvings. (Nowadays, printing techniques have passed from the Typo era, with lead-cast letters, to modern four-color offset printing techniques).

The artist draws a picture of a stork perched on a bamboo branch, bent and soft as if about to break, with a gloomy look as if it was about to fall into a pond; the pond's water surface was calm, and a night scene in the miserable autumn. Looking at the image and six verses of the poem again makes me feel sorry for the fate of the stork. In the eyes of people, or poets, the stork is the image of a Vietnamese mother. The stork's diving body represents the embodiment of a mother in the countryside, working hard night and day to raise her children... The image of a Vietnamese mother is even more astounding when living overseas. Indeed, our Vietnamese mothers

---

8 Cut the hair short, almost shaved in the front, gradually increasing in the back; it looks like a horseshoe shape.

9 In the past, if people wanted to celebrate a death anniversary in the village, they had to apply for permission.

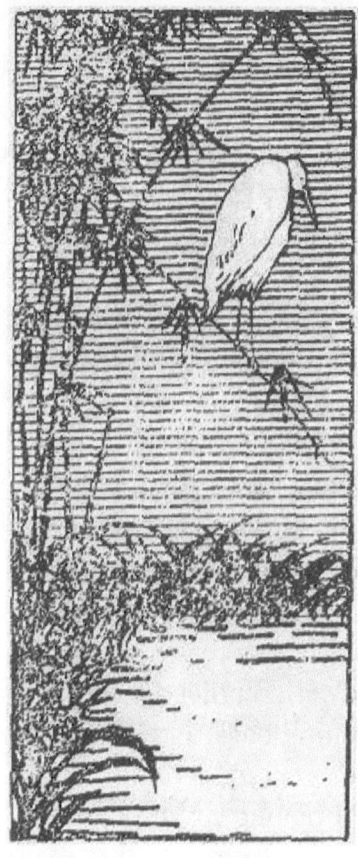

A picture of a stork perched on a bamboo branch (Lecture Elementary Course)

are lovely; saying that is no exaggeration.

Let's delve into the author's words, where the story of the stork is used to convey a profound moral lesson:

"The stork, despite falling into the water and being caught by people who intended to slaughter it, requests to be cooked with clear water so it can die cleanly. That is akin to a poor person who ventures into business and faces losses or accidents yet always maintains a pure heart and refrains from unclean actions. This tale of resilience and purity of heart is truly inspiring and worthy of our admiration."

The stork, the mother, always lives for her children and dies for her children:

> *If you cook, please cook with clear water*
> *Don't stir up turbid water; that hurt the little stork's heart."*

Through the image of a stork, Lecture Elementary Course teaches students moral lessons and metaphors of eternal value.

Each person has a different situation and position in society; each of us has an image of a mother that we cherish: Teacher Tử Lộ's mother, King Tự Đức's mother, the countryside mother in the works of Phạm Duy, Y Vân's mother in the song Mother's Heart. Whether your mother or my mother, they are all the same. Is there any difference between a King's mother, a mandarin's mother, a wealthy mother, and a poor mother?

When I was a child, at the end of the month, the end of the trimester, or the end of the year, I would bring my school report card, grade book, and honor book home for my mother to sign. My mother would sign in a convoluted manner, sometimes with a cross. My mother is like that, but she loves her child endlessly and takes care of her until she dies. Looking back, later, I became successful, rode a car with a driver, and lived in a house with servants, but I still liked having my mother cook for me, and I liked sleeping next to my mother every time I visited my homeland!

Our Vietnamese mothers all want to *"keep the hearts pure,"* that is the life lesson I cherish and carry with me on my journey.

Now, my mother has passed away at the age of 92, a long life. At my mother's funeral, I placed a pair of red candles on the altar to celebrate my mother's longevity. I said "goodbye" before leaving the funeral in front of hundreds of relatives, friends, and family, with tears streaming down my face...

Reread the folk song *"The Stork goes out to eat at Night"* with its moral meaning and mother's teachings: *You must keep your heart pure* as a memory of my mother and the mothers of those who, unfortunately, no longer have mothers.

On this Vu Lan*, as I revisit the Lecture Elementary Course, the image of the stork stirs up memories of my mother, a feeling I know many of you share. I rejoice for those who still have their mothers by their side. Let's all stand together and share the pain of those who have lost their mothers. And let's all strive to keep our hearts pure, a testament to our love for our mothers.

*Reflecting on the Vu Lan season
in foreign lands, 2004*

---

*The full moon day of the seventh lunar month is Vu Lan Holiday, commemorating dead parent, and for those who have living father or mother, they should know that they are the happiest.

7. MY HOMELAND IS THE MOST BEAUTIFUL

In the past, the people we were born with only knew where they were. Some people have not learned what a province or market town is all their lives! Since the French came in the Southern region, only two or three villages have had a market. When I was a child, my mother took me to the market, and I was so happy because children being taken to the market is something "horrible."

Back then, no concept of "civilization" or "urban" existed. People living in rice fields and farmers are called "countrymen" in the French, which means rustic, ignorant, and poor, which means "market"!

In my homeland, people often send others to the market every morning, meaning they see their neighbors go to the market and ask them to buy things for them. It's normal for someone to go to the market and buy things for two or three people. Going to the market, in addition to purchasing cooking items, my mother often buys cakes for my sisters and me. "Bánh" is a general term for snacks sold at the market, such as sticky rice, cassava, sweet potato, bánh bèo, bánh bò... and rarely bought in Chinese shops such as green rice, candies, dry cake... because it is expensive. Nothing is happier for a country child than watching their mother come home from the market. As soon as the mother arrived at the gate, the child screamed: "Má's home! Má's home!" Nowadays, there is a saying in folklore that "Longing like longing for Má coming home from the market"; that's what it is.

Growing up, our generation lived only with fields, rivers, canals, village ponds, communal houses, pagodas, bamboo bridges, and monkey bridges. The countryside scene left a deep impression on our generation. It was bold and unforgettable, and I consider it a homeland.

You live in a garden all year round with remarkable green trees and citrus fruits hanging heavy on the branches. When you grow up, you wander here and there, wandering around for life, but you must remember your Homeland. Some friends live in a dry field called "đồng." The field here is dry land; the river water does not reach it. Farming depends on the rainy season, and growing vegetables and cabbage in the dry season is watered with well or pond water. They grow close to the eggplant garden, vegetable garden, mustard greens, or betel nut garden. Some friends live all year round on boats, on sampans, traveling up and down rivers and lakes, And I grew up in the water fields. The river water is six months fresh and six months salty; we are used to catching crabs, tiny crabs, and watching ducks.

Each of us has a Homeland in our hearts. The song "Each person's homeland is only one" is like that. Remembering the old years, I went to the province to study and only got home on weekends. Cycling on the village road, passing two or three turns, looking in the distance, my neighborhood appeared... my heart was filled with indescribable joy!! That feeling grew more profound when I later went to Sàigòn to study and work. The farther I go, the more I visit here and there, the more I love my homeland.

Now, re-reading the Lecture Elementary Course, I feel sorry for the authors and understand the gentlemen's love for their homeland. Description of the story "The Traveler Returns Home": I would like to quote here:

> *"A person traveled to many places. Many people knew his relatives, friends, and neighbors the day he returned home. A friend asked: You visited the mountains and water and must have seen many beautiful scenery. So where do you think is the most interesting?"*
>
> *The tourist replied, "I have seen many beautiful scenes, but nowhere makes me more moved and happy than when I return to my homeland and see the old fence and mud wall of my father*

and mother's house. From the bamboo bush in the corner of the garden, the winding road in the village – everything evokes indescribable feelings for me."

The author chose "The Most Beautiful Homeland" for the above article. The reading exercise about "The Traveler Returns Home" is simple but has a profound educational meaning. Anyone can understand it, and it is appropriate for our feelings.

The Traveler Returns Home replied, "nowhere makes me more moved and happy than when I return to my homeland
(Lecture Elementary Course)

After more than fifty years, re-reading the Lecture Elementary Course in the context of being an exile is exceptionally touching. How profound is the sentence, "The homeland is the most beautiful?" The Homeland in each of us is very small and straightforward and doesn't need anyone to paint it, tell us to love it, or ask us to remember it, but why does it forever occupy a prominent place in our hearts and force us to recognize and love it?

Is it the Homeland that has raised us and helped us live forever in the Vietnamese way? So, no matter where I am, I still find my Homeland, Việt Nam, the most beautiful.

Vietnamese families are often large, including grandparents, parents, and children. Three generations living under the same roof is an unforgettable image in the hearts of each Vietnamese person, especially expatriates!

Nowadays, even in our country, the scene of family reunions at dinner or in the evening is still a challenge! When recalling this activity, young people are amazed and see it as a fairy tale, while adults feel regretful!

Welcome to the Lecture Elementary Course Preparatory class, where we delve into the fascinating world of Vietnamese meal traditions and family activities. One such intriguing session is 'Evening at Home,' which we will explore in detail.

"After dinner, it was just getting dark. The lamp was hanging in the middle of the house.

> *Dad was sitting reading the daily newspaper. He was sitting down, looking at books, or doing homework. Mom and sister were sewing needles and needles. Next to them were two little brothers who were doing homework. Listening to her tell fairy tales, sometimes giggling together happily."*

Vietnamese people's dinner has always been the main meal before resting and going to bed so they can work early tomorrow.

There are three meals a day.

Breakfast is called a filling meal because it is a light meal. Today, it is called breakfast. In fact, in the past, people usually ate rice for breakfast and were full so they could go out to work in the fields. However, this meal is simple. They call it breakfast in America, meaning it's a quick, easy meal.

Lunch is often eaten in the fields or at work. It is usually more substantial than in the morning but still includes a salty dish with rice. It is wrapped in banana leaves or areca leaves, often peeled or broken off tree branches to make chopsticks. People at home eat lunch even though they have bowls and chopsticks.

The main meal is dinner (evening meal). Everyone gathered. Grandmother or mother prepares a complete meal with better-quality dishes, such as soup, vegetables, and salty dishes.

What do our meals always include?

First and foremost, rice. However, the Vietnamese culinary journey is still ongoing, with rice alone. It's a gateway to a plethora of essential dishes, such as:

- ***Salty dishes:*** made from fish, shrimp, dried fish, fish sauce...
- ***Soup*** is a liquid dish with water, made from shrimp, fish... with vegetables. Six Provinces' civilians love vegetable soup and sour soup, eating it to cool their stomachs and help them sleep.

Raw vegetables are a filling dish that is very popular with Southerners and easy to find everywhere. These are cucumbers, melons, mustard greens, and especially kale. Vegetables can be boiled or eaten raw.

Our meals are not just about sustenance; they are a reflection of our unique cultural practices, especially soup. Vietnamese people eat rice with soup during meals, a tradition that sets us apart from our Chinese

The main meal is dinner (evening meal). Everyone gathered.
(Drawing in Lecture Elementary Course)

Family gathers together after dinner.
(Drawing in Lecture Elementary Course)

and Western counterparts. Chinese people eat rice after eating soup (or porridge). Westerners and Americans, on the other hand, eat soup before the main meal.

After finishing the meal, the family gathers around the lamp for activities.

Oil lamps hanging or placed on tables or boards are all oil lamps; previously, they were tamanu (*dầu mù u*) or coconut oil. In the past, hanging lamps were often bought in China and sold by boat traders from China.

During that era, while newspapers were primarily centered in Sàigòn, Hà Nội, and other central provinces, a different form of storytelling thrived in the rural areas. This form of storytelling, deeply rooted in the cultural fabric of Việt Nam, allowed people to immerse themselves in the tales of *Lục Vân Tiên, Thạch Sanh Lý Thông, Lâm Sanh Xuân Nương, Phạm Công Cúc Hoa*, and even Chinese stories.

Talking about "Sewing needles and threads," let's go back to the old days of sewing and dressing. In addition to cooking, women also have to know how to sew. So then, before going to her husband's house, her mother bought her a "sewing basket" including a needle, thread, scissors, thread... The sewing basket was made of bamboo and woven "long fashion" like a rice basket. But smaller. Some people even make lids and legs for sewing baskets, which look very beautiful and seem to be very precious.

As time passed, new innovations began to shape how we dressed, reflecting the dynamism of Vietnamese culture. Elastic bands, a modern convenience, were introduced much later. In the past, pants were secured with fabric strings. However, when the demands of work required a more secure fastening, coconut strings were used, showcasing the adaptability of Vietnamese dressing practices.

During that era, the traditional '*áo dài*' was fastened with fabric knots, but later, squeeze knots became the norm. Women's blouses, known as pocket shirts, featured two pockets and were worn underneath. The '*Bà ba*' shirt, a popular choice, initially used shell buttons and later transitioned to latex buttons with four or two holes. Interestingly, men's shirts were buttoned on the right side, while women's and girls' shirts were the opposite, buttoned on the left side. Can you guess the reason behind this unique cultural practice?

When I was a child, everyone loved listening to my grandmother tell fairy tales, myths, and legends, but now that I'm old, I still remember how beautiful they are!

The "family gathering in the evening" scene is rare, especially in foreign countries. Everyone in the dark house stares at the TV, watching Chinese movies and Cải lương (Vietnamese operetta). Children often go into their own room when they grow up a little. Life is busy; many must work and go to school at night. Everyone has their key, goes their way, and lives in privacy even though they are under the same roof!!

Rereading the Lecture Elementary Course, the article "Evening at Home" reminds us of the social and family scene of our people in the early 20th century. At that time, at the transition of time, the family scene still existed, like two sentences. Six-eight poems are as follows:

> *Boys read books and recite poems*
> *Girls weave, sew, and embroider.*

Along with "sewing and embroidery," Vietnamese women cook for the family.

As mothers and wives, Vietnamese women have, over the years, put their souls into cooking, mixing, and creating. With their heart and love for their husbands and children, and with their intelligence, they have created dishes that are new, suitable for the times, and ideal for the family.

The country opened toward the South, and with their resilience and adaptability, Vietnamese women created

Boys read books. and recite poems / Girls weave, sew, and embroider.
(Drawing in Lecture Elementary Course)

"Southern dishes" to suit local activities and specialties, a testament to their creative resource.

Our eating has been elevated to a national culture, which we call culinary culture. Vietnamese women have created a cuisine unique to Vietnamese culture and distinct from China and the French. Even though these influences have been present for a long time, they are a source of pride in our cultural heritage.

When speaking:

> *When eating, watch the pot, sit and watch the direction*

Or

> *The greeting was higher than the feast*

We see a hint of culinary culture created by women. Today, half of Vietnamese people living abroad are women and are the authors of Vietnamese culture in foreign countries through cuisine.

Concluding the lesson "Evening at home," Lecture Elementary Course wrote:

> *"Working hard during the day, but at night the whole family is so full and reunited, I thought there was no better joyful scene..."*

In addition to dinner, "evening at home" is a cultural beauty of Vietnamese people, no matter where they live.

The 'evening at home' is not just a routine for family members but a heartfelt reunion after a day of hard work to sustain their lives. It's a tradition upheld, if not every night, then at least once a week, to keep the family bond strong. The 'evening at home' is a time to cherish, a time to reconnect, and a time to appreciate the hard work of each family member.

Girl sitting at loom weaving fabric
(Drawing in Lecture Elementary Course)

The responsibility falls heavily on women. Only women can become wives, mothers, and grandmothers from the age of a girl. That's why we call it 'sacred vocation.'

The 'divine vocation' of women, a role that was prevalent in the past, continues to be upheld in Vietnamese society today. Whether you are the wife of an ordinary citizen or a prince, living in a village or a forbidden palace, the essence of this vocation remains the same. It's a testament to the enduring values of Vietnamese culture.

The precious virtues of Vietnamese women, such as Diligence-Manners-Speech-Morality (*Công-Dung-Ngôn-Hạnh*), go beyond the "Four Virtues" framework and no longer have the binding or strict nature of feudalism but belong to nature- The qualities of Vietnamese women. Diligence-Manners-Speech-Morality is the essence of Vietnamese women, making every mother voluntarily teach them to her children as if it were a mission.

In contemporary Vietnamese history, there was Queen Nam Phương, the wife of King Bảo Đại. She deserves to be a Vietnamese woman. She followed Mrs. Từ Dũ, making women radiant and glorious and knowing how to care for her family.

I want to quote a portion of Mrs. Nam Phương's message to the world, denouncing France's return to Việt Nam after Bảo Đại's abdication but rarely heard anyone mention it:

"Việt Nam was liberated from the slavery of the French and Japanese empires.

When he surrendered, my husband, former Emperor Bảo Đại, declared, "It is better to be a citizen of an independent country than to be the King of a slave country." I have also mercilessly given up the privileges of a queen, standing side by side with women to help preserve the sacred independence of our country. At this moment, blood is flowing on the land of the South, the cradle of my childhood. Countless lives were burned by the criminal greed of some French colonialists supported by some British troops, acting contrary to the instructions of their allies. I call on all those who have suffered because of the crimes caused by the new great war (World War II, 1939-1945) to take action to end the nameless violence that is raging in my country.

On behalf of 13 million Vietnamese women, I request all my friends of the country of Việt Nam to speak up and demand the freedom and rights that everyone aspires to have to preserve the country. Civilization has its values

Queen Nam Phương, the wife of King Bảo Đại.

so that the world's youth do not doubt the idealism they have learned.

By appealing to your governments to intervene and establish a just and genuine peace, you are fulfilling a human responsibility and accepting our fellow citizens' gratitude. Your government's intervention is a crucial step towards the freedom and rights we seek for Vietnamese women."

Mrs. Vĩnh Thụy
Former Queen Nam Phương[10]

In short, Vietnamese women have always played an essential role in contributing to protecting and building the country, including building culture.

With love and perseverance, women are the decisive factor in fostering family life, just like the spirit of the lesson in the Moral Teaching Textbook: "At home at night."

---

10 Excerpt from "Today's Knowledge" translated in the book HCM-Abd-EL-Krim et Cie authored by Renaud by Guy Boussac, published in 1949 in Paris, France.

8. A DELICIOUS MEAL

Vietnamese people have always valued meals, especially family meals. Usually, at dinner, everyone gathers together, so it is! The father went to work in the fields with a buffalo and a plow. I go to school. Mom stays at home and takes care of the housework. That is the main meal.

During these meals, it is a cultural norm to maintain a peaceful atmosphere. Siblings and parents refrain from scolding or arguing, fostering a sense of harmony and respect.

God's strikes avoid the meal time.

The proverb speaks to the spirit of respect for family meals.

Lightning strikes, called God's strikes, often occur at the beginning of the rainy season in the countryside. People say that when eating rice, God will never beat you (?)

Here is a typical family meal description:

> *"Not long after Mr. Ti came home from school, his father carried the plow and led the buffalo back home."*
>
> *That is a family dinner. There was a father who went to work in the fields with a buffalo and a plow. I go to school. Mom stays at home and takes care of the housework. A typical scene of an ancient Vietnamese farmer family."*
>
> (Lecture Elementary Course)

Vietnamese people used to eat three meals a day. We eat in the morning to go to work; lunch is a meal that is usually not full of people, and dinner is the main meal because it includes everyone.

Returning to my homeland, I was struck by the stark contrast in eating habits. The traditional three meals a day in the countryside have been reduced to two, with breakfast often skipped. It's even more extreme in the city, with many people only eating one meal daily. This significant shift in our daily routines is a testament to the changing face of our society.

The author of the Lecture Elementary Course described the mealtime precisely like ours at home:

> *"The rice is cooked. Mom and sister served it on the bed. The whole family sat down to eat. Red rice, vegetable soup, nothing fancy. But the rice was sauced, clean bowls, hot soup, clean*

chopsticks, everyone." Eat and drink well and be complete."

In the Six Provinces region, a unique dining tradition was observed. Families would gather around planks, known as 'counter boards' or 'horse boards, 'to share their meals. The food served on brass trays that aluminum ones later replaced was a sight to behold. In the past, the trays were made of wood, intricately carved, and a testament to the craftsmanship of the time.

When I was a child, my parents assigned me to clean the dishes for dinner. Every time like that, we must count the people in the house to avoid "eating without enough bowls."

That was due to the proverb: "If you eat rice, you will have fewer bowls. If you pound rice, you will have more pestles." Borrowing the phrase "eating rice but lack of a bowl" here is to recall my childhood memories of always missing a bowl and chopsticks when serving rice because I didn't know how to count.

In the South, seeing anyone eating red rice is a rarity. The least preferred is white rice. However, if you have the means, you can indulge in the aromatic delight of fragrant rice. Rice, especially fragrant rice, holds a special place in Vietnamese culture. Our old country meals are rich in fish, shrimp, and homegrown vegetables. However, our meal might need more meat, fat, and sugar, so it was easy to get hungry quickly, but we had to eat a lot of rice in return.

This love for rice is so strong that when Vietnamese people migrate to America, they often long for the familiar taste of rice, a taste that carries with it the memories of home and family.

You'll notice a unique seating arrangement at the dining table. Men often sit 'cross-legged', while women and girls adopt a 'one leg folded, one leg propped up' posture. This traditional way of sitting, once considered unattractive, is a testament to the enduring nature of Vietnamese culture, still prevalent among Vietnamese communities in America.

The tray is also used to steam fruit, make betel on wedding days, or make sticky rice. It is worn on the head when going to the communal house to worship Kỳ Yên, a deity that is close to every family and plays a significant role in Vietnamese communal life.

Vietnamese chopsticks are often made of bamboo. They are produced in batches, resulting in uneven pairs. It is essential to compare them when using them to serve rice.

However, industrially produced chopsticks are now more uniform. The countryside is named after the white cotton tree, which is traditionally used to cook sour soup with goby fish. The long fruits of this tree hang parallel to each other, resembling chopsticks, hence its name "pairing the chopsticks."

Hence, the conclusive definition of a *"Delicious Meal"* requires a pleasant and close family atmosphere:

> *"Especially when parents and children are in harmony, a reunited family gathering makes the rice and vegetable oil taste even better."*
> (Elementary Course)

That's right! A "delicious meal" is considered such because of the food's taste and the atmosphere of unity during the meal. Harmony is vital when sharing a plate and sitting at the same table.

Vietnamese people have a standard bowl of fish sauce, a dipping sauce that the whole family uses and shares. This practice reflects the Vietnamese lifestyle of "sharing" and "togetherness" within the household. Some argue against this practice due to hygiene concerns of dipping sauce that the whole family dibs and shares. Dipping into a bowl of fish sauce is a Vietnamese lifestyle, expressing the spirit of "sharing" and "togetherness" in the house. Some people say they should leave it because it's unhygienic.

Writer Vu Hanh wrote the book *Noble Vietnamese* in the 1970s, excessively praising the bowl of fish sauce in Vietnamese meals. Knowing that he wrote according to the political needs of the time and to avoid censorship, he recorded it as a translation by A. Pazzi, an Italian writer.

Around meals, Vietnamese people have many proverbs and folk songs that are very meaningful and profound, such as:

> *- Watch the pot when you eat, watch the direction when sitting*

- You lose your appetite when you're full; you lose your mind when you're angry
- Eat on the same tray, lie on the same mat.

Observing the rice tray during meals reveals the enduring legacy of our ancestors' way of life, preserved and celebrated today. This unique 'Vietnamese style' is not just a tradition but a testament to the cultural richness and depth we must strive to uphold.

When we enter someone's house and look at the meal, we can understand whether that family's lifestyle is harmonious and happy.

The 'family meal' is not merely a culinary event but a profound expression of our people's way of life. It symbolizes a lifestyle rooted in the values of family and clan, a testament to the author's wisdom in imparting this knowledge to past students.

In the United States, there are households where the concept of 'family meals' is not given the same reverence as in Việt Nam. They do not embrace the significance of 'family meals' in fostering familial bonds and cultural preservation. That's regrettable!

9. GRANDMA LULLS HER GRANDCHILD

"Summer noon, the sun was shining, and the wind was quiet. Inside the house, outside the alley, it was empty and silent. In a side wing, the grandmother held her grandchild in her arms. They lay on the hammock, rocking them repeatedly, a creaking, creaking, rhythmic sound."

At the beginning of the article: *"Grandma lulls her grandchild,"* the author describes the summer afternoon scene in her old homeland; what a peaceful and reminiscent scene it is! Rereading the summer afternoon scene in the countryside makes many of us recall our childhood, especially those who lived in that situation when they were children.

It was summer noon, the sun was shining, there was no wind on the street, the trees stood still, and no single person was in the alley. The scene was so familiar.

The grandmother held her grandchild in her arms. They lay on the hammock. Grandma lulls her grandchild.
(Drawing in Lecture Elementary Course)

Back then, in the countryside, in front of the house, people often left a jar of water for passersby to quench their thirst during the dry season. If you stop on the way and drink a bucket of rainwater, there's nothing better than that.

The image of a carefully covered water jar is next to a small coconut shell with a handle specially made for drinking water in the countryside, which is rarely seen anymore! I don't know who had that idea, but water jars are everywhere in the Six Provinces countryside in front of the house; the layout is the same.

Every Vietnamese family has a hammock. I don't know when it arose, but the hammock is associated with our lives as something "noble" beyond its function of resting.

The hammock is associated with childhood, the elderly, men, women, and especially country girls. The feeling of lying in a hammock, swinging, reading books, reciting poems, or rocking a baby is magical, and no one dislikes it.

In the past, our Kings and mandarins also liked hammocks: Kings slept in royal red hammocks, mandarins slept in hammocks with stretchers carried by people, and the student who passed the exam was, *"He goes first in the hammock, and her hammock follows behind..."* Going first opens the way for you. The "his hammock" or "her hammock" and especially the "Mandarin's hammock" have a whole entourage, shouting for people to get out of the way. In the South, those soldiers are called "road announcing" soldiers.

Hammocks also rushed along with the Tây Sơn army to fight the enemy, transport the wounded, or take the sick to the province to find a doctor.

In front of the house, often left a jar of water for passersby to quench their thirst.
(Drawing in Lecture Elementary Course)

The hammock is tied to two house pillars. Underneath, it is often lined with mats and torn pads to prevent "the earthy vapor" from rising and affecting the health of the person in the hammock. Some people hang hammocks above their family's bed or on planks for comfort and convenience.

Let's talk about the materials used to make hammocks in the southern countryside in the past.

In the past, ice silk hammocks were popular, better than durable wooden hammocks, and the best were bamboo hammocks, which were both strong and bug-free.

The top of the hammock is meticulously crafted, with a hole to insert a piece of bamboo known as a 'glove.' When attached to a string wrapped around the house pole, this glove is what we call hanging a hammock; in the North, it is called hanging a hammock.

Swinging in a traditional hammock was a sensory delight. The rope rubbing against the house pillar created a familiar 'creaking, creaking' sound, adding to the experience. However, with the advent of nylon hammocks, the scorching heat and the absence of the swinging sound took away the joy of hammock lounging!

When buying hammocks, people often counted how many taus (threads of hammock) the hammock had to avoid negative numbers and raise children and grandchildren quickly.

In the scorching summers of the South, we would often hang hammocks in the garden under the cool shade of trees. Nothing quite like the bliss of a midday nap in a hammock, a tradition passed down through generations.

Lecture Elementary Course describes a grandmother and a grandchild lying around the side of the house, both relaxed and able to see the outside scenery, which is very common in the countryside.

The old houses in Six Provinces were mostly thatched and built in the shape of the letter Dinh; the upper house is next to the lower house. Every home has a front porch, a back porch, and even a left-right porch. It blocks rain and sun from entering the house, and the awnings on both sides are also used to store agricultural tools and household tools such as jars jars, mills, rice pounders, flour mills, and plowing tools...

> *"She sang, she lulled:*
> *Tiny sleeper! It would help if you slept for a long time,*
> *Your mother went to plant the field and has yet come back."*

The grandchild listened to the softly chant; she seemed asleep, and the grandma looked like she had half-closed eyes.

> *"Yes, tiny sleeper! Your sleep shall be profound,*
> *Your mother works hard day and night."*
> (Lecture Elementary Course)

No one taught anyone, but Vietnamese mothers in the past knew many lullabies to their children. The mothers sang along to the "creaking" sound of the hammock, one verse after another, with ups and downs and rhythms like artists.

When children are very young, they have sharp memories that can catch the singing and voices of adults. When they hear lullabies, they are silent, doze, close their eyes, and gradually fall asleep.

In America, we now see young mothers lulling their children to sleep with soft music from a cassette on their children's bedsides.

Let me remind you of some old lullabies from Đồng Nai - Sài Gòn- Six Provinces in the past:

> *- Nhà Bè's water flow is parted into two streams,*
> *Anyone who returns to Gia Định or Đồng Nai will return.*
> *Come here into this strange land,*
> *Even the chirping bird is scary; the fish is frightening.*

> *- Your boat's nose is red, its sides are wide,*
> *Up above from Gia Định came down to the garden to visit me.*

> *- The wind blows, the wind pushes to the fields to eat crabs,*
> *Back to the river to eat fish, then to the pond to eat melons.*

> *- Supposed that the wood bridge got nails,*
> *The bamboo bridge sways; it's bumpy and hard to walk on.*

> *- Guess how many legs you have?*
> *The Bridge Ô has how many spans,*
> *And how many people does the Market Dinh have?*
> *The Market Dinh sells boys' shirts,*
> *Market Trong sells thread; Market Ngoài sells needles.*
>
> *- The bird Bìm bịp call that the water is rising,*
> *Trading without profit, rowing tiredly.*
>
> *- The bottom column has hanging lamps*
> *The water flows, and the light vibrates.*
> *I love you too much, so dearly,*
> *Do you know if your father and mother are content?*
>
> *- Mom wants to marry me back to the garden*
> *Eat boiled pumpkin flowers and melons in soup!*
>
> *- To build a garden, you must dig a ditch*
> *As a man with two wives, you must love them equally.*
> *You transport rice to Công*
> *Back to Vàm Nao against wind and storm;*
> *the sails are broken!*

Southern lullabies often adopted the Six-Eight words' poetry but sometimes have variations, such as the Six Provinces has the back-chat folk-singing.

In addition to the content about the love between a man and a woman, lullabies also express the people's misery, especially the plight of women at that time.

Vietnamese women, especially mothers, in addition to giving birth to children for their husbands, also have to take care of all the cooking and sewing for the family.

Women are also involved in farming. They do some lighter work than men: Weeding, transplanting rice, and harvesting rice next to a man, one sun, two dew. The scene of women planting rice and harvesting rice in the fields is often depicted in books, stories, and paintings.

In Six Provinces, except for the Đồng Tháp flooded area, other places use the transplanting technique everywhere. In the South, no one is called a transplanter but a transplanting laborer, a seedling laborer, or a plowing laborer.

Transplanting is the stage of putting seedlings into cultivated fields. With the right hand, people use a utensil called *"cây nọc"* or *"cây nọc cấy"* to poke holes; the left hand plucks a few cloves of seedlings to plant!

Depending on the variety of rice, people plant it thickly or thinly and grow it small or large. Early rice is harvested large and planted thickly; seasonal rice is picked and planted sparingly.

"Cây nọc" has two parts: the body is octagonal like a banana shoot, the lower part is pointed and made of wood, and the handle is made of a light tree like a tree *"quau,"* piercing at the trunk like a cross.

The laborers carefully care for the *"cây nọc"*; anyone rarely lends them. After transplanting and washing, people put the *cây nọc* on their backs and go home.

Transplanting is the stage of putting seedlings into cultivated fields. (Drawing in Lecture Elementary Course)

The scene of a grandmother keeping her grandchild at home so her mother can work in the fields is normal during seasonal activities in the countryside.

At that time, there was no cow's milk, so people gave children rice, water, and porridge mixed with sugar, and some mothers took their grandchildren to ask for "sharing milk" when their mother was away.

> *My baby sister is thirsty for milk and sucks her hand.*
> *Who feeds her with some sharing milk? I'll feel so grateful.*

I'm reading the article *"Grandma lulls her grandchild."* I miss my old homeland so much! At that time, our people were all poor, living day to day, caring for each other, and growing up like that.

In such a typical situation, no one feels miserable! So the images of thatched roofs, buffaloes, plows, and country mothers are poetic and lovely and will be left in our hearts forever.

Nowadays, people's lives are better when it comes to taking care of a grandchild or child breastfeeding, and there is no longer the scene of the grandmother lulling the grandchild and asking for the "sharing milk" so that the mother can plant and plow.

> *"Tiny sleeper! You should sleep for a long time,*
> *Your mother went to cultivate the deep fields*
> *and hasn't returned yet."*

Does this belong to the past?

As time passes, the beauty of my homeland, with its thatched roofs, buffaloes, plows, and country mothers, remains alive only in the verses of poetry and the notes of music.

But anyway, is it better than nothing?

10. ONE WHO GOES, ONE WHO STAYS

Upon revisiting the article "One Who Goes, One Who Stays" from the book Lecture Elementary Course resonates deeply with the experiences of Vietnamese individuals living abroad, making it a highly relevant piece of literature.

In the Introducion, the authors write:

> *"After the meal, my father, mother, brothers, sisters, and even family members sent me off to the riverbank, where the boat was docked.*
>
> *A wave of despair washed over me as I exited the house. From my earliest memories, home was a place of joy and comfort. But now, faced with separation, I realized it was a different world out there."*

Throughout history, our ancestors chose to stay rooted in their birthplaces. They led quiet, leisurely lives, rarely venturing beyond their villages and families. It was a closed, self-sufficient existence like one life seamlessly flowing into the next. However, with the advent of Western influence, our society was shattered: life became more bustling, people more active, and there was a surge in trade and travel. This societal transformation is a crucial aspect of the cultural context in 'One Who Goes, One Who Stays. '

The article *"One Who Goes, One Who Stays"* speaks to that context.

During those times, long journeys were undertaken primarily by water and on land, where the roads were treacherous, and horse-drawn carriages were the mode of transport. That made leaving home for an extended period a significant event, requiring the entire family and guests to bid farewell at the riverbank and boat dock.

At that time, the boat station was just a riverbank, different from the organized boat station or station like today. Wealthy people all bought boats and hired friends to row here and there. Boats traveling long distances often had a roof with a place to eat and sleep. Ships in the South were usually painted red on the nose with two eyes: black and white irises on the sides.

My boat has a red nose and a white body
Up from Gia Định, I come down to the garden
to visit you.

That custom, which originated in Gia Định, was a result of the initiative of Mr. Nguyễn Cư Trinh (1716-

1767), the Chief of Staff in Gia Định at the time (1751). He painted the nose of the boat red to prevent accidents, a practice that significantly influenced the local boat station customs. The custom also served as a deterrent to river theft, a prevalent issue at the time.

Mr. Nguyễn Cư Trinh's ancestral homeland was in Nghệ An, then moved to Thừa Thiên and became a Mandarin under Lord Nguyễn Phúc Khoát (1738-1765), guarding Tuần Vũ Quảng Ngãi.

When Chân Lạp King Nặc Nguyên colluded with the Trịnh army to attack Lord Nguyễn, he was sent to lead the Gia Định army to go to Nam Vang to punish him. Nặc Nguyên lost and offered the two palaces of Tầm Bôn and Lôi Lạp to atone for his crimes.

Remembering the old days, before leaving home, mothers often told their children to eat "three grains of rice" to fill their stomachs, a tradition that became a habit over time. That is just one of the many cultural traditions and habits related to boat stations that have left a deep and unforgettable impression on our lives.

As for myself, I remember when I first passed the exam to enter the second grade of the Provincial School (fourth grade today), before the first day of school, holding a bag of clothes in my hand, walking away with the desire to stay... My mother took me to the new school. The bridge has been crossed, but mother and little son didn't want to say goodbye yet! It was the first time in my life I had to leave home. On weekends, when

I visit home and my mother on Saturday, there's nothing better than being happy.

That scene, "some stay and others go," and "the scene of separation," are shared experiences among all of us elementary course students. We all go through it; we all feel it.

> *"walking away, looking back from the roof, the steps, the path, the bushes, the grass – everything makes me attached and unusual.*
>
> *Everyone wished me smooth sailing, peace, and health when the ship took off. The boat had gone far, but I stood and looked back, looking until I couldn't see the house anymore. Oh, how sad the parting scene is!"*

(Lecture Elementary Course)

Even though we know we will return when we leave, every farewell scene evokes a bittersweet feeling of sadness and attachment. At that moment, the pond bank, the jar, the water jar, the hibiscus fence, the entrance... They all stir up a deep sense of nostalgia as if they have a soul of their own.

Is that the "homeland" of each of us? A question that lingers in our minds, stirring up emotions and memories.

For Vietnamese people who have left their homeland, the memories of the separation of many families in the situation of "Some stay, some go" are so great, so deep, that it is difficult to erase from memory.

All family members sent me off to the riverbank.
(Drawing in Lecture Elementary Course)

Looking back on the days I spent preparing to cross the border, I still feel my heart broken! I had to bring my mother to Sàigòn to stay with me as if trying to hold on to something about to be lost.

That morning, my mother still made a sumptuous meal, but no one in the family could eat, even though everyone sat at the table, eating to make her happy! I drove out of the house without daring to turn back, but I knew my mother would stand in front of the door, watching for a long time.

"Oh, the scene of separation, how sad"!

The ending to the song "Those Who Stay, Others Go" evokes endless pain in my heart – the heart of each of us, people far from home.

Now, the rivers and seas are connected. We all have the opportunity to visit the place where we "came from", walk on the path to the old house, look back at the old garden, and find familiar dishes again.

Or, in the early morning, go to a familiar Sàigòn street corner coffee shop, sip a steaming cup of freshly brewed coffee, listen to the gossip around you, and look back to the past.

For overseas Vietnamese, the scene of separation, when some stay and some leave, is a profoundly emotional and indescribably painful experience. Leaving the homeland is a massive separation for us, a heart-wrenching goodbye with no hope of returning.

In the past, the Elementary Course lecturers, often seen as the bearers of knowledge and wisdom, thought it was a temporary farewell when they talked about the farewell scene. But now, the significant departure of the nation without anyone to send them off is a situation that is difficult to label or describe adequately.

After thirty years, we have acquired everything the country offers regarding material wealth and knowledge, but hundreds of thousands of people still choose to return to Việt Nam every year.

Why?

We leave with everything we can bring, but how can we get our homeland, even though "each person only has one?"

Returning to our homeland is to truly live with what we left behind when we left:

- Drinking a cup of coffee on the streets of Sàigòn, looking at the flow of people going back and forth, not used to it, but why do I find Sàigòn so lovely?

Returning to Trà Vinh, the experience of visiting Bà Om pond is not just about its physical attributes but about rediscovering the love of the countryside, the memories of being a student, and the journey of learning to love!

Returning to An Giang, visiting the market house is a chance to buy a jar of salty pork intestine, a piece of pork belly, a package of vermicelli, and a few herbs. Then, it's time to gather with old friends and prepare a bowl of salty intestine with vermicelli, just the way we like it. Enjoying a hot buffalo horn chili while discussing life's ups and downs is a joyous occasion that brings us closer together.

For the ladies, a visit to Bà Chúa Xứ in Sam Mountain or Chùa Bà Pagoda in Bình Dương on the full moon day is a cherished tradition. Whether listening to the men discuss fate or seeking blessings for prosperity, these unique cultural practices are a source of pride and a reminder of our shared heritage.

As time passes, the distance from home only seems to intensify the feeling of nostalgia.

Fifty years later, re-reading the song 'Someone Stays, Someone Leaves' in the context of April 30 is a poignant reminder of the bittersweet nature of our memories.

Our shared experiences are unique to us, and how the lecturers we had in elementary courses could realize them. They are part of our community's identity, and no one outside of it can truly understand.

As a child, I read "Someone Stays, Someone Else Goes" to cultivate a love for the homeland and family and practice and train myself to be independent, challenging, and unafraid of difficulties.

Now that we are living in a foreign land, re-reading the article "Those who stay, others will leave," is it to feel compassion for the lost family and compassion for our children and grandchildren to see if they will still be in the same state of mind as us?

Fruit market group.
(Painting by Trường Mỹ Thuật Gia Định, 1910-1920)

11. GOING TO THE MARKET TO PAY

One "quan"[11] of good tiền[12] to take away,
She bought what she couldn't count.
At first, I bought three tiền of chickens,
One and a half tiền of sticky rice and three coins of betel.
Come back and buy six tiền arecas,
One and a half tiền for meat, ten tiền for vegetables.

That is the first part of the folk song *"Going to the market to pay,"* which was included in the book Lecture Elementary Course and taught to elementary school students in the past.

The money in the card is our old money before the West came. Before 1725, old Chinese copper coins

---

[11] *Quan*: is a string of 10 ancient coins.
[12] *Tiền*: equal to 1/10 of the quan. One Tiền: equal to 60 zinc coins (string coins)

Money from copper coins
(Drawing in Lecture Elementary Course)

were circulated in ĐàngTrong, which were often broken by people to be made into use, so they were lost. In 1725, Lord Túc Tông Nguyễn Phước Trú (1725-1738) ordered more bronze coins to be minted for use. While illegal lead, cast iron, tin, and pirated coins are still circulating among the people, they are called lousy money to distinguish good money from copper coins.

The opening sentences of the folk song "Going to the Market to Pay" show us the everyday life of the ancients, how our ancestors ate and drank at that time, and how the market traded.

Today, a trip to the market rarely reveals anyone buying betel and areca nuts. The custom of chewing betel leaves, once common, is now almost exclusively reserved for weddings. This shift in cultural norms, the fading of a once deeply embedded tradition, evokes a sense of loss for a part of our cultural heritage.

When I was young, my grandmother often went to the market early in the morning to buy a dozen pairs of yellow betel nuts and a few thick white areca nuts. Yellow betel is old betel, with yellow leaves, high concentration, and fragrance (while green betel is young betel). White areca nuts have an acrid taste but are not as harsh as red areca nuts (red areca nuts are often used to dry).

Later, my mother also had the habit of chewing betel, and her style of choosing betel nuts was a graceful dance reminiscent of her grandmother's. She chewed the betel, cut off the betel tail, rolled it into a round shape, and then put it in her mouth to chew, a sight of elegance and tradition.

How can future generations feel like the old generation, the Elementary Course generation, in which betel, areca, and market stories became a part of life?

Where will the fate of the areca and betel gardens of Hóc Môn and Bà Điểm go next?

That's why it is said that culture is constantly changing: Culture reflects life. When life changes, culture changes.

So why say culture must be preserved?
- Those are two sides of life, especially human life.

Nowadays, the *betel piece* is no longer *just the beginning of the story*. It has evolved, becoming a symbol of love between husband and wife, a mark *of respect in wedding ceremonies*, grandparents' birthday celebrations, and ancestor worship ceremonies. It's a testament to our culture's ability to adapt and endure.

Preserving culture is preserving those things; indeed, no one doesn't want to protect culture. Therefore, in America, during wedding ceremonies, everyone tries to get at least three pairs of betel nuts and fresh areca nuts to worship at the altar and for two children to bow to their ancestors, which is cultural preservation.

The Course continues with how we ***"Go to the market to pay"***:

> *"Is there anything you can't figure out?*
> *One and a half coins of ordinary rice, six coins of fresh tea.*
> *Thirty coins of wine, my dear,*
> *Thirty coins of honey, twenty gold coins.*
> *Two bottles of fish sauce.*
> *Twenty-seven or fourteen lest you become suspicious.*
> *Twenty-one coins of tea powder,*
> *Ten coppers for a bunch of bananas is even one coin."*

In Vietnamese culture and daily life, the market holds a significant place. The image of a woman, mother, wife, and daughter is almost always associated with the market and cooking, as the saying goes:

> *A wise man looks for a wife in the crowded market*
> *A wise girl finds a husband among the soldiers.*

In ancient times, the market was the primary place Vietnamese women could reveal their true nature.

Despite having few opportunities to go out into the community, they communicated, managed money, and honed their skills in choosing products to prepare meals for the entire family.

"Thirty coins of wine, my dear."

It shows that she is genuinely a wife who loves her husband very much and cares about his hobbies.

In the past, when I was a child, I saw my grandmother take care of every drink for my grandfather, ordering family members to scoop out a bowl of delicious, freshly cooked sour soup for him when he came home late from work... I didn't understand. Then my mother continued to do that later...

What is that called?

If it's not vocation or love, then what is it?

In the article "Going to the Market to Pay," we should briefly discuss our people's market.

No one has said when the market existed or its history, especially where the Vietnamese market came from, but the image of the market is. Please take note of the following text:

There are many types of markets. First were the "primitive markets," the "squatting markets," and the rural markets. The primitive markets were spontaneous. Due to natural needs, people came together to exchange, later known as buying and selling.

Then, there are fixed markets with curb roofs; each individual, in their designated section, contributes to a

A grocery store in town.
(Drawing in Lecture Elementary Course)

vibrant community, fostering a sense of connection and making transactions a seamless experience.

Then, there are fixed markets with curb roofs; each individual, in their designated section, contributes to a vibrant community, fostering a sense of connection and making transactions a seamless experience.

Coming to the French, the market was built with cages made of iron ribs, brick pillars, and tiled roofs and handed over to the village to manage, with a fee for space (selling tax).

> *Guess how many feet a centipede has?*
> *The train has a few beats; how many people does Dinh market have?*

The train has a few beats; how many people does Dinh market have?

Dinh market, provincial market, city market... are more significant in scale, crowded, and noisy, so my grandparents used to say "crowded like a market" or "noisy like a market."

Our local market is a treasure trove, offering a diverse range of goods: fresh shrimp and fish, a colorful array of vegetables and fruits, everyday necessities like needles and threads, bottles of cumin oil, and even complete herbal medicine.

Going to the market is not just about shopping; it's a cultural experience. You can listen to *Vọng Cổ* singing, recite poetry, or watch some kung-fu '*Sơn Đông Mãi Võ*' performance to selling goods, which is now called advertising and marketing...

Unmarried women and women with complex relationships go to the market to show their palms to people or tell their fortunes.

Many women and girls also go to the market to eat. They try a bowl of noodles, a cake, a crunchy fried cake, "*bánh xèo,*" etc.

No matter where you are, whether in a large or small market, a rural market, or a provincial market, your Vietnamese market is truly a unique image, a beautiful "civilization."

Visiting a Vietnamese market is an opportunity to immerse yourself in a sensory feast. You will see people bustling about, smell the enticing aroma of food, the pungent scent of shrimp and fish, hear the lively chirping of vendors, and catch snippets of conversation and confession from the people around you.

Almost everyone who comes to the market is open, confiding, and considers each other friendly, even though they have just met or gotten to know each other. The market is also a place to exchange information, where information is collected from everywhere and will be quickly transmitted to every home within a day.

Visiting a Vietnamese market in my homeland is a truly unique experience. It's not just a place to buy and sell but a communal space that brings the community together. With its vibrant sounds, flavors, colors, and specialties, the market evokes deep emotions and fosters a profound sense of connection among people, making you feel like you belong to it.

The afternoon market is full of star fruits and lemons,

Market, it's not just a place to buy and sell but a communal space that brings the community together.
(Painting by Trường Mỹ Thuật Gia Định, 1910-1920)

Many beautiful girls around excite him.

Indeed, the Vietnamese market has always attracted us and made each of us more or less nostalgic.

The Vietnamese market is no longer just a place to buy and sell; it has become a place to convey and share our feelings, fostering a sense of empathy and understanding among its visitors.

The folk song *"Going to the market to pay"* tells a side of real life in the past that is almost no longer there. Today's domestic market has also changed a lot over time, giving you a sense of Vietnamese culture's rich history and evolution.

The vibrant wholesale markets like An Đông Market, Bà Chiểu Market, and the night markets such as Chợ Lớn Mới offer a unique and lively shopping experience, integral to the beauty of life. However, even abroad, we often find ourselves confined to the sterile and impersonal aisles of the American supermarket.

We are overseas. On the weekend, we go to the supermarket (American market). The husband pushes the cart, the wife holds a list of things to buy, pushes it to the cashier counter to pay, and receives a thank-you sound. The supermarket atmosphere is dry, isolated, businesslike, emotionless, and heartless!

But what should I do? That's how life and culture change.

For life to not be emotionless, we may have to return to our Vietnamese family foundation. Rereading Lecture

Elementary Course, the lesson "Going to the market to pay" immediately sees the old way: we still have to rely on women, not because they go to the market or cook rice, make delicious dishes for husband, children, or family. However, because of the need for love and care from the wife and mother through family meals. The family meal is not just a meal; it manifests love and care, a tradition that binds us together.

If the supermarket and the family meal are insensitive, then the family routine must be broken and lost.

Hundreds of thousands of Vietnamese, including many ladies, return to their homeland every year. Is it because they are so bored with the "emotionless supermarket?"

When the ladies return to their homeland, they all want to go to the market to enjoy the past's flavors and buy a few things to cook their favorite dishes every day. And with that, the ladies are satisfied.

So we can see that despite living far from home and from the local culture, Vietnamese women still see their vocation and want to preserve it.

12. SOGGY RAIN AND CHILLY WIND

Our country is in the tropical climate zone, near the sun (equator), and is always hot and humid. In the South, there are two seasons, Rainy and Sunny, while in the North, there are four seasons: Spring, Summer, Fall, and Winter. As children, we all liked to shower in the rain, whether in the countryside or Sàigòn. Showering in the rain leaves us with many lovely and unforgettable memories.

In the United States, if you live in Southern California, you rarely see rain, and no one especially likes rain, let alone showering in it.

The Lecture Elementary Course, there are contains two captivating lessons about rain: *"Soggy Rain and Chilly Wind"* and *"The Rain."* These lessons, which are used as reading lessons for Preparatory (Fourth grade) students, delve into the cultural and historical significance of rain in Việt Nam. They will open your eyes to the fascinating world of rain in Việt Nam and its importance in the country's history and literature.

When parents and grandparents who have experienced the 'two seasons of rain and sunshine' in the South or prolonged rain and chilly wind' in the North reread these lessons, they will find their memories. These lessons serve as a bridge, connecting the young generations in the United States to their roots and helping them understand the weather patterns of their homeland.

Understanding your country and homeland means more than just knowing about the weather. It means delving into the rich tapestry of Vietnamese history and literature, a duty and responsibility we all share our grandparents' lives. As the young generation, you have a crucial role in preserving this rich cultural heritage.

> *"In the winter, the countryside landscape looks lonely and sad when there is soggy rain and Northern chilly wind. Out in the fields, it's cold (in the South, it's called frozen hands and feet), and we only occasionally see people plowing or harrowing. Everyone worked together in groups, not chatting happily like when it was warm. In the village, the roads are deserted and ankle-deep in mud. There was no sound around me; I only heard the wind blowing into the bamboo bushes, and the water dropped to the ground."*
>
> ("Rain and wind" - Lecture Elementary Course)

The scene of farmers working in the fields and plowing under the wind and rain is not just challenging but also a testament to their resilience. In the past, people did not have raincoats, so they had to use raincoats and conical hats to protect themselves from the rain.

The north wind, "gió bắc," a chilly breeze from the north, starkly contrasts the warm climate of the South. While the farmers' attire in the past is a mystery, it's safe to assume that the women no longer don four-piece dresses or cannot rely on sweaters for warmth. The image of trudging through ankle-deep mud or plowing in the rain with the north wind is a foreign concept to the South.

A man wearing raincoast walking in then soggy rain and chilly wind.
(Drawing in Lecture Elementary

In the South, it was the end of the lunar year. The weather was chilly, enough for the ladies to "wear the maid's scarf," and the older men wrapped bandanas around their necks to keep warm. At this time, the rice in the fields had already "run the leaves," the rice started to weigh down, and the farmer prepared to reap.

When it comes to the bandana in Six Provinces, everyone knows it, even if you are not a local "gardener," but few people know about its origin. Some people believe that the Khmer people of Six Provinces were the original owners of the bandana. In contrast, others believe that since the early days of the brand-new land reclamation, our ancestors created the bandana to suit the harsh weather conditions. It can be used to bathe and wipe the face, especially for women to wrap their hair neatly and for servants to cover their heads for warmth. The bandana also serves a practical function in preventing mosquitoes from biting, a testament to its ingenuity.

Over time, the bandana with white/black squares transformed into one with white/red squares, a fashion statement for country girls who wore it loosely to flirt with unmarried men. This transformation of the bandana into a symbol of flirtation is a fascinating evolution.

> *"The weather was hot, the leaves of the trees and grass were silent, and suddenly a cool wind blew. Looking up, I saw that the clouds had darkened a corner of the sky. Everyone said that there was going to be a heavy rain."* On the street, people are walking around, everyone walking quickly to get home soon or to find shelter from

the rain. Inside the house, everyone calls out clothes, blankets, rice, and straw; you have to dash everywhere. There are unusual noises. Only in the fields, he plows, and she plants; they are calm work because they have already prepared enough hats and coats."

"The Rain" that the Lecture Elementary Course describes above reminds us of the scene of showers in the South, which a Northern poet who migrated to the South described as "suddenly raining, suddenly sunny."

It's raining, a woman brings things into the house from the yard.
(Lecture Elementary Course)

When I was a child, my grandparents said that if you look at dark clouds close to the horizon, it's about to rain, but clouds that aren't close to the horizon, called "broken clouds," mean it won't rain. This experience seems always to be true.

The scene of plowing in the rain in the South is typical because the weather is not cold, and the water in the rivers and fields is hot when it rains.

As a child, I was assigned to pull straws to cook rice when it rained. When it rained for several days, I had to pull out straws to dry in the yard and sit and watch for rain.

During the rainy season in the South, people often have to wait until the sun shines to dry clothes, firewood, straw, and especially rice before grinding it so it doesn't get crushed.

The most exciting thing that I still remember today is showering in the rain, showering throughout the rain, and when the rain stopped, I quickly changed clothes. My hair was still wet, my mouth trembled, and my lips were purple and black. I ran into the kitchen to warm up. My mother gave me a hot, fragrant sweet potato. I ate too quickly and didn't have time to swallow – how delicious!

There were times when there was heavy rain and strong winds, and Mother was not at home; the sisters closed the doors and lit a fire to keep the house warm and to ward off ghosts. The kitchen, with its comforting warmth and the smell of cooking, was our sanctuary during stormy weather, making us feel safe and secure.

Then, memories of rain will grow with age, and we will have many other memories.

These are the memories that fill us with anticipation and joy, especially the ones of going fishing in the rainy season. They bring back a flood of nostalgic emotions and a deep sense of connection to our past.

In my homeland, there are many traditional folkways of catching fish that everyone in the family knows: fishing with a trap and a net, fishing with a pole, fishing line, fishpot, net, etc. These shared practices create a sense of unity and belonging in our cultural community.

Our ancestors passed this down from their experience living on the rivers and water of Six Provinces, from ancient times until now, and thanks to that, we have fed the people and increased the family's income without spending anything.

According to instinct, after heavy rains, the Increased rainwater floods rivers, canals, and garden ponds; field fish lie somewhere in the summer, trying to find a way to cross the water and swim back up to the fields. In the countryside, it's called the "fish up." The village called each other, picked up the basket, took it out to fish soup, and scooped it up to bring it home.

Catching perch across the shore and water during heavy rain is fun. Going out in the rain to catch perch across the water is the happiest festival brought by "showers." After that, the fields began to flood, which people called "flooding," and the harvest began.

Also, the scene of putting on a leaves coat, a patched shirt, and a conical hat, going to the fields to remove nets to catch perch and silver carp, visiting some fishing rods, or visiting some roofs placed on the side of the dike, or watching the standing water. There's nothing better than pouring it into the trap to catch Goby fish to cook porridge.

One night, instead of bringing the fish home, I stopped by someone's hut, lit a straw fire to cook a pot of porridge, and the other kids went somewhere to pick up a handful of herbs, a few chili peppers, and a few cloves of onions – and that's it – a pot of hot Goby fish porridge. A few foraging young kids, while sipping porridge and learning to drink rice wine, we talked about the story of "Monkey King" and felt wonderfully happy.

Reread '*Soggy Rain and Chilling Wind*,' recall the lyrics of the song 'The Rain' that once echoed through your homeland, and feel a pang of nostalgia for the people who toiled in the rain and sun, plowing, catching shrimp, catching snails…

How can children today in foreign lands experience rain as we did in the past? Rain is often understood as a scientific phenomenon here, devoid of the emotional and cultural significance it holds in our homeland.

Parents must share their experiences with their children, especially regarding rain. By recounting their memories of rain in their homeland, they can make rain in a foreign country more than just a scientific phenomenon. They can make it a part of their shared history.

If anyone remembers the rain, remembers the perch wading through the water in the rainy season, I suggest you go to a restaurant and order a plate of fried perch or a bowl of gourd soup cooked with gizzard perch to come back alive. The past… Although the scent of the past has faded somewhat!

PART III

COUNTRY AND PEOPLE

1. *Education in the past*
2. *Year-round agriculture work*
3. *The buffalo*
4. *My village*
5. *My village temple*
6. *The old-time soldiers*
7. *Sir Phan Thanh Giản*
8. *Indochina Railway*
9. *Sàigòn City*
10. *Literature & poetry not good*
11. *Thank Heaven for timely sun and rain*

"In the past, students of Confucian education took the exam to get the diploma granted by the King and become mandarins. The exam had two departments: the Multi-Province and National Assembly."
(Drawing in Lecture Elementary Course)

1. EDUCATION IN THE PAST

The "Exam courses," about taking exams while learning Chinese characters, are one of the exciting but exceptional subjects that the Lecture Elementary Course of the Preparatory class has an object lesson for young students.

According to history, our country has been autonomous since the reign of Ngô Quyền in 939, and since then, we have taken Chinese characters as the base to use in transactions and studying for exams. When the new country gained independence from China in the early days, the dynasties still had to deal with many upheavals, so they needed more time to organize studies and exams. The work of learning was often undertaken by Buddhist monks because, at that time, only they were knowledgeable about Chinese characters (Monk Vạn Hạnh was King Lê Thái Tổ's Confucian teacher since childhood). During the Lý dynasty, King Lý Thánh Tôn

(1023-1072) had the initiative to establish a Temple of Literature to worship Confucius and teach the princes. That was the Thăng Long Temple of Literature, today is the Hà Nội Temple of Literature.

In 1243, the King officially established Quốc Tử Giám, the National Royal School, to educate the children of Kings and princes, and later extended this privilege to the children of mandarins and then the brilliant children of the commoners. In 1237, Hồ Quý Ly sought King Trần Thuận Tôn's approval to appoint mandarins to administer education in localities such as Lộ, Phủ, and Châu. Minh Mạng, in particular, played a significant role in organizing education and exams. He introduced the concept of 'education officers' at the town, government, and district levels, who were responsible for coordinating studies and selecting exam candidates.

The educational structure is like that, but what about the teaching?

Back then, students needed to have the luxury of attending school daily. Instead, they displayed remarkable dedication by gathering monthly in their districts to listen to lectures on scriptures and stories. This practice, known as 'the teaching of the book,' was a testament to their commitment to learning.

Also, periodically every month, they had to practice writing assignments called "literature practice" for the teacher to grade (sometimes, they had to take the papers home to do).

Some Confucian instructors teach at private homes among the people and villages. They are Confucian intellectuals who did not pass the exam (called "poor" Confucianists), and they can also be people who passed the exam but do not want to become Mandarins (called "hidden" Confucianists). Many Confucian scholars passed the exam, participated in the official government, enjoyed benefits, and had social status (called "successful" Confucianists).

According to Lecture Elementary Course:

> *"In the past, students of Confucian education took the exam to get the diploma granted by the King and become mandarins. The exam had two departments: the Multi-Province and National Assembly."*

In 1396, King Trần Nhân Tôn established strict exam rules that underscored the rigidity and structure of the examination system. The student who passes the Province Exam (*thi Hương*) this year will attend the National Assembly Exam (*thi Hội*) the following year. The results of these exams determine the student's academic standing, with those scoring over 50 points earning the prestigious title of a Bachelor's degree (Double-Bachelor is the one who passes two Province Exams, but the scores are under 50).

The student who passes the National Assembly exam (*thi Hội*) is called a Doctor or Scholar (*Tiến Sĩ*). During Minh Mang's reign, besides having a doctorate listed on the main board, they also had a Deputy doctor degree

(*Phó Bảng*) listed on *Secondary board*; from there, we have the qualifications of Deputy Doctor (like Deputy Doctor Nguyễn Can Mộng, and Deputy Doctor Nguyễn Sinh Sắc.)

The Primus Doctor (*Trạng Nguyên*) was the person who passed first in the Assembly Exam (*thi Hội*), which King Trần Thái Tôn established in 1247 (premier doctor, deputy doctor, second deputy: the three highest achievers in the Assembly Exam).

In 1374, King Trần Duệ Tông organized the Assembly exam (thi Hội) in the King's yard, which became known as the royal Hall exam (thi Đình) from then on.

> *"King Lê Thái Tôn wanted to make the examination more solemn, so he established the "honorific announcement" and "honorific home-returning" rules for scholars. He also had the scholar's name engraved on the stele built at the Temple of Literature in Hà Nội (Văn Miếu Hà Nội), later built by the Nguyễn Dynasty in Huế.*

(Lecture Elementary Course)

Let's listen to Sir Phan Kế Bính's description of the announcement ceremony during the Nguyễn Dynasty as follows:

> *"The day the graduates' name announcement is called the day of the grand naming ceremony was held at Thái Hòa temple. The mandarins dressed in court uniforms were divided into groups to stand before the Emperor. Then, the responsible Khâm Mạng Mandarin reported on the exam, and the proctors summoned the*

The day the graduates' name announcement is called the day of the grand naming ceremony. (Lecture Elementary Course)

new graduates to come forward. The soldier entered the dispatch house, served the King's orders, and rewarded each person with clothes and hats. After the Rites Ministry official, the new doctoral graduates went to the dispatch house, followed the King's orders, and awarded each set of gowns and hats. The officials of the Ministry of Rites led them to kneel and line up in front of the dragon yard. The announcer held the book to announce the names."

"Afterward, a significant sign has been prominently displayed in front of the Phú Văn edifice for three consecutive days, marking a momentous event.

After the announcement, the committee had a banquet at the Rites Department office, giving each graduate a brooch. That morning, school officials and new doctoral graduates dressed in court uniforms and paid tribute to the royal banquet. After consuming the banquet, each new graduate must give a speech of thanks.

Under the guidance of the esteemed officials from the Ministry of Rites, the supervisors, and the new graduates in mandarin outfits, riding horses, and covered by parasols, they embarked on a glorious journey into the royal garden to admire the blossoming flowers, then to the East citadel gate to enjoy the city."

Phan Kế Bính
Việt Nam Customs
(*Indochina Magazine, new edition, no. 41*)

Examinations in the past intended to select talented people to serve the country. The King conferred the degrees of Bachelor, Deputy Doctor, Doctor, or Primus Doctor through selection exams.

Those who pass the exams would devote themselves to helping the country and its people, a sacred duty that included social, intellectual, and political aspects. The position of Confucian scholars in our ancient society lasted nearly ten centuries.

Today, intellectuals and highly educated people are respected in society but are no longer highly regarded as a vocation like the Confucian scholars of the past.

Regarding the Primus Doctors (principal graduate or *Trạng Nguyên*), from the Lý dynasty to the Trịnh dynasty, there are 56 primus doctors:

1. Lê Văn Thìn, year 1075
2. Mạc Hiển Tích, year 1085
3. Bùi Quốc Khải, year 1185
4. Nguyễn Công Bình, year 1213

5. Trương Hanh, year 1232
6. Nguyễn Quan Quang, year 1234
7. Lưu Miễn, year 1239
8. Nguyễn Hiền, year 1247
9. Lý Đạo Tái, year 1252
10. Trần Quốc Lặc, year 1256
11. Trương Xán, same year 1256
12. Trần Cố, year 1266
13. Bạch Liêu, same year 1266
14. Đào Thúc, year 1275
15. Mạc Đĩnh Chi, year 1304
16. Đào Sự Tích, year 1374
17. Lưu Đức Kiệm, year 1400
18. Nguyễn Trực, year 1442
19. Nguyễn Nghiêu Từ, year 1448
20. Lương Thế Vinh, year 1463
21. Vũ Kiệt, year 1473
22. Vũ Tuấn Thiều, year 1475
23. Phạm Đôn Lễ, year 1481
24. Nguyễn Quang Bật, same year 1481
25. Trần Sùng Dĩnh, year 1487
26. Vũ Duệ, year 1490
27. Vũ Tích, year 1493
28. Nghiêm Hoàn, year 1496
29. Đỗ Lý Khiêm, year 1499
30. Lê Ích Mộc, year 1502
31. Lê Nại, year 1505
32. Nguyễn Giản Thanh, year 1508
33. Hoàng Nghĩa Phú, year 1511

34. Nguyễn Đức Lương, year 1514
35. Ngô Miên Thiệu, year 1518
36. Hoàng Văn Tán, year 1523
37. Trần Tất Văn, year 1526
38. Đỗ Tông, year 1529
39. Nguyễn Thiên, year 1532
40. Nguyễn Bỉnh Khiêm, year 1535
41. Giáp Hải, year 1538
42. Nguyễn Kỳ, year 1541
43. Dương Phú Tư, year 1547
44. Trần Bảo, year 1550
45. Nguyễn Lương Thái, year 1553
46. Phạm Trân, year 1556
47. Đặng Thì Thố, year 1539
48. Phạm Đăng Quyết, year 1562
49. Phan Quang Tiến, year 1565
50. Vũ Giới, year 1577
51. Nguyễn Xuân Chính, year 1637
52. Nguyễn Quốc Trình, year 1659
53. Đặng Công Chất, year 1661
54. Lê Danh Công, year 1670
55. Nguyễn Đăng Đạo, year 1683
56. Trịnh Huệ, year 1736

Briefly, the way of studying and taking exams that the Lecture Elementary Course discusses in the article "Exams" is to train people to understand the morality of saints and sages. Depending on the circumstances, they are known, hidden, or cold, but their style is always exemplary and virtuous, setting an example for society to follow.

Our country has a tradition of using literature as its basis. Thus, it is called a country with 4,000 years of civilization because it has talented people and cultural history books.

As we advanced, embracing the national language, the exam style transformed. However, the wealth of talented scholars and the diverse, rich tapestry of cultural history books continued, underscoring the depth and diversity of our cultural heritage.

An official in the past, he had a servant by his side.
(Lecture Elementary Course)

2. YEAR-ROUND AGRICULTURE WORK

Our country has long relied on agriculture as the main occupation. Growing rice is the main thing; other agricultural products are secondary. Our people have always mainly eaten rice. Some areas have a rice shortage, so people must eat cassava, sweet potatoes, and corn. So, our grandparents had a saying:

Vital for rice, violent for money.

A grain of rice, a grain of rice, our parents taught us to value and call it a pearl. Kings always have policies to encourage agriculture, advising people not to leave fields fallow:

Don't leave the fields fallow, everyone:
So many feet of dirt, so many feet of gold.

Our people's deep-rooted connection with agriculture is evident throughout history. The knowledge of working in the fields has been passed down from generation to generation, with parents taking the lead in training their children and grandchildren. This 'father-to-child' learning method has been a cornerstone of our agricultural tradition.

Now, let's delve into the Elementary Course Lecture that explores the fascinating world of 'year-round agriculture work'.

> *"January is the month of fun.*
> *In February, plant beans, potatoes, and eggplants.*
> *By March, the beans are old*
> *We go, pick them, and bring them home to dry.*
> *In April, I go to buy cattle and buffaloes.*
> *Let us prepare for the May season.*
> *In the morning, take the rice out to soak the seeds*
> *When it sprouts, we will take it out.*
> *Carrying the burden, and I sow my fields,*
> *When it's time to plant, we'll spit it out.*
> *I'm about to borrow money from a cultivator,*
> *After the transplant, I return to rest."*
>
> (*Year-round agriculture work is excerpted, from the Lecture Elementary Course*)

Agriculture work is described according to the cycle of days and months in a year, and it involves adapting to changes in weather. Our country is in the tropical monsoon region, with heavy rain and high humidity. The North has four seasons, while the Central and South only have two: rainy and sunny. From the article, we know that that is the work of Northern farmers.

January (lunar month) is the month to celebrate Tết (New Lunar Year) and have fun at temples, and everyone wants to go to something other than work.

In the North, many additional crops are grown to be self-sufficient in family food. When potatoes are a side dish mixed with rice, it is called mixed food (*ăn độn*). Only after 1975 did people in the South know this way of eating mixed food.

In the South, farmers produce other crops, mainly for sale, in addition to growing rice. They know how to specialize in farming because the land is significant, and people need to be more sparse. So, in the South, there is Bến Tre, the land of coconuts, and Cổ Cò, the land of watermelons. Trung Lương is the land of plums, Hóc Môn is for vegetables, Bà Điểm is the land of betel and areca, etc.

Mr. Phạm Quỳnh, Nguyễn Bính, and Nguyễn Hiến Lê visited the South and wrote extensively about its life and fields, showing that the region has long had specialized farming.

The buffalo in the sentence "*April we go to buy buffaloes and cows*" also highlights a unique feature of our ancient rural life. Buffaloes are the primary means of production; the owner of a buffalo must register in the village and commune and be issued a buffalo registration book, similar to the boat registration book. When the French invaded the Southern region, a veterinary clinic was established to protect buffalo herds and exploit the French plantation areas. In addition to being registered,

Bucket type with stretcher, hung by three poles, slapped by one person (Drawing in Lecture Elementary Course)

buffaloes also got stamped on their butts (brass marks, grilled red, stamped on the buffalo's butt) to prevent the buffalo from being stolen. Our old law severely punished people who stole buffaloes, sometimes forcing them to be exiled to another country.

Planting rice is a labor-intensive process, particularly in the South, where it is often done by hand. Only large

Buffaloes are the primary means of production
(Drawing in Lecture Elementary Course)

landowners have the resources to hire workers for this task. The planting labor is gathered early in the morning when the ringleader blows the horn to signal the start of the day's work. The middleman is responsible for coordinating the planting on the landowner's behalf. Their role is crucial, as they distribute the labor to the fields. The farmer typically provides food for the transplanter.

Agriculture's work, Lecture Elementary Course continues to describe the popular following folk song:

> *"The rice grain has been cleared,*
> *The water in the fields is low; the flood is one or two.*
> *"The high fields are covered with a roped bucket*[1]
> *For the low fields, you have to place two handle buckets*[2]
> *Wait until the rice has rice stalks*
> *Now, I will pay for the laborers.*
> *How long until October,*
> *We took the sickle*[3] *out into our field*
> *We reap the harvest and bring it home*
> *Dry it, clean it, and they're done."*

---

1 The roped bucket (*gàu giai*) bucket type has ropes on both sides with two people holding the slap.
2 Bucket type with stretcher, hung by three poles, slapped by one person
3 The cutting ring was used to harvest rice. It was made of a light wood "quau" shaped like dogwood. One end was used as a handle, the other was easy to pick up the rice, and it had a sickle for cutting.

In the morning, take the rice out to soak the seeds
(Drawing in Lecture Elementary Course)

When it's time to plant
(Drawing in Lecture Elementary Course)

We reap the harvest and bring it home
(Drawing in Lecture Elementary Course)

After transplanting, the farmer's work moves to phase two, which involves caring for water and grass, waiting for the rice to bloom, and harvesting.

In the South, there are two types of rice fields: one is field type, where rice plants only survive on rainwater, and the second is upland fields (mostly) that mainly get river water. Type 2 is found in Hậu Giang, while in Tiền Giang, there are alternating fields and plantations.

Agriculture fields often use a system of canals, irrigation ditches, or drainage ditches, so they do not use buckets. When the fields are in a drought, they must use buckets to bring water into them. In the South, the fields are flat and have no slopes, so they are often slapped with a bucket. In the countryside, the wars usually use ponds and ponds to catch fish in the dry season near the Lunar New Year because the ponds are bottomless.

Ripe rice is harvested with a picking ring (called a sickle in the North). After harvesting, the rice is bundled and transported to the houseyard by boat or cart, carried with a rice-carrying pole, which is like a pole but with thinner double-heads for carrying the rice sheaves. Some people have one bundle on each end; some strong people carry two bundles. Therefore, people in the Southern region often use the image of a carrying rod to refer to a person who is not steadfast and follows every direction to gain advantage (double-headed lever). The rice grains are separated from the rice straw by being trampled by buffaloes, then dried, using a fan (far from the rice fan), blowing clean; also, some places use the wind to slightly "blow" it clean.

Grain rice, a communal effort, is stored in baskets in dry places. Many people, united in their work, toil in the fields, and rice is stored in large warehouses made of wood boards called rice storages. In short, a farmer's work, a shared responsibility, mainly involves growing rice throughout the year, from sowing to harvesting. Early rice ends in the lunar October, and summer rice ends in the lunar November and December.

Rice, the sustenance of our people, feeds the people; whoever has a lot of rice is rich. Our society, deeply rooted in this staple, is ranked as follows: Scholars, Farmers, Workers, and Merchants. Peasants, the custodians of this wealth, are second only to the Si (mandarin class, educated people).

Agriculture, the backbone of our society, was our people's main occupation until the 21st century. The life of a farmer, a stark contrast to the hustle of the industrial society in America, is complicated but generally more leisurely. So those in their sixties cannot forget the sentence:

"*January is the month of enjoyment*" in the folk song "*Farm work all year round*" of Lecture Elementary Course, like regretting the leisurely days of the past!!

3 THE BUFFALO

In rural life, the buffalo is the animal closest to humans. Among the six animals, six have meritorious services to humans, of which the buffalo is the leader. Therefore, in the Lecture Elementary Course Preparatory class, the authors wrote two articles about the buffalo:

- *Herding Buffaloes,* and *The Buffalo*

In the article *The Buffalo*, the authors describe as follows:

> *"Buffaloes are larger than cows and have more strength; their hair is black, hard, and sparse; sometimes they have white hair, their eyes are dull, their horns are big and curved."*

As a child, I was fortunate enough to experience the thrill of riding a buffalo. It was a memory that I cherish to this day, a testament to the unique bond between humans and these magnificent creatures.

Growing up, I sometimes came back to my homeland to visit on weekends or summer vacations, and my friends would let me ride a buffalo out to eat. Sometimes, wading through fields and crossing rivers was extremely interesting and memorable.

The white buffalo is called the "stork buffalo" and is very rare. Curved and pointed buffalo horns are used to fight each other; in the North, it is called buffalo battle (*chọi trâu*). Every year, buffalo battles occur on the 10th of the 8th month - "*No matter who trades or sells anywhere, they come back for the buffalo fights on the 10th of the 8th month.*" There are buffaloes whose horns curl down like the horns of goats or cows, called "buffalo *cui*." Large male buffalo is called "buffalo *Cổ*" *(Cổ: Mông Cổ, belongs to the Mongolian buffalo breed)*. Southern farmers usually have buffaloes in every household if they work in large fields or on many fields; some landowners have hundreds of acres.

In buffalo herds, there are usually more male buffaloes than female buffaloes because male buffaloes are solid and work well. Raising a female buffalo has the advantage that it gives birth to little ones, giving more pulling and plowing power. Each female buffalo usually gives birth to one baby buffalo, which is called a calf. When buffaloes and calves are raised for a few months, their owners pierce their noses to tie them, which is called piercing *vàm*. (A girl who has just grown up and has not done anything worthwhile for her parents, but follow a boy is called a pierced lass!)

Buffaloes chew their own cud again like cows. They eat quickly and swallow quickly, but when it's time to lie down for lunch or at night, they extrude eaten food from their stomach to their mouth, then chew again until smooth. Buffaloes are gentle and like to live close to people.

In the countryside, we have to burn straw to have smoke at night to prevent mosquitoes from biting the buffaloes. In some places, mosquito nets are made for the buffalo to sleep inside. In other areas, people dig a lagoon for the buffaloes to lie down at night so the mosquitoes don't bite them. That lagoon is called a buffaloes swamp.

In the past, each time people drove a herd of buffaloes from one village to another for plowing, often by river, it was called buffaloes free moving[4] (*len trâu*). Sometimes, a herd of hundreds of buffaloes can be seen going far away day and night.

> "*Buffaloes are used to plow fields, pull carts, or cover sugar cane. Buffalo meat is less delicious than beef. Buffalo skin is used to cover drums or make shoes. Buffalo horns create knife handles, medicine tubes, and combs.*"
> (Lecture Elementary Course)

The buffalo, a historical figure in our agricultural landscape, is crucial in shaping our fields. It pulls the

---

4 Sơn Nam's popular story "*Buffaloes Free Moving Season*" ("Mùa Len Trâu") was filmed domestically by the French-Vietnamese director Nguyễn Võ Nghiêm Minh.

plow; it pulls the harrow. Two buffaloes work together in the South to plow, while a single buffalo takes on this task in the North. After plowing, they diligently harrow the soil, breaking it up and smoothing it out. They transport bundled rice and bags to the yard, boat, and bus stations. The buffalo also aids in road construction by pulling covers to press sugar cane and even treads rice. Their work, often described as extreme struggle, is a significant part of our agricultural history.

Our people value the buffalo, so no one kills it to eat it unless the buffalo is sick or injured and cannot work or the buffalo is old. Thus, famous composer Viễn Châu wrote a somber Vọng Cổ piece (Vietnamese operetta) named "The Old Buffalo Life," sung by the renowned artist Hữu Phước, talking about the fate of a buffalo that cannot work when it gets old, sounds tragical! Everything in its body will be consumed, made into instruments or even garments.

Buffaloes are used to plow fields
(Drawing in Lecture Elementary Course)

The province Gò Công has a specific dish of buffalo meat stir-fried with coriander leaves and coconut milk.

In the countryside, buffalo horns are blown to gather labor or cut into pieces to make the "bell-bowl" (*mõ*). The strong buffalo bell-bowl has a small sound but is clearer than the bamboo and wood mù u bell bowls, so they get used for worship, ceremonies, and at home. Buffalo skin covers the drum and makes leather. In Chợ Lớn, in District 6, there was a Lò Da (Leather Manufacture) next to Lò Gốm (Pottery Manufacture).

Every farming family that raises buffaloes entrusts a hired buffalo herder, usually a server, meaning a boy between ten and eighteen years old, his parents often allow them to live with landowners for five or ten years to earn some money or acquire land to cultivate. The role requires the young herder a sense of responsibility and independence to take care of the animals.

A folk song about buffalo herding, found in Elementary Course:

> "*Who said herding buffaloes is miserable?*
> *No, herding buffaloes is very fun...*"

Herding buffaloes, cows, and ducks, but only buffaloes herding is prevalent and dreamily described in poetry. The image of a boy wearing a conical hat, holding a bamboo whip, and swooning on a buffalo's back like a fairy is not just exciting, but also an adventure in itself. The youngster may look like some Taoist trainee, but he is also a daring explorer in the vast fields.

Buffaloes like to walk and live in herds, so they rarely get lost, and unlike cows, they don't need to wear a jingling bell around their neck.

As the afternoon sun begins its descent, the herder guides the buffalo back to the barn or secures each one to a stake. With its unique technique called buffalo wick (*niệc trâu*), the art of buffalo tying demands precision and skill. When tying a buffalo to a pole, the rope must be tied tightly, akin to a dog's collar, instead of a loop or knot, so the rope does not slip. The buffalo wick rope, crafted from the resilient fibers of coconut peanuts, is a testament to the herder's skill and the buffalo's strength, and it's a sight to behold.

A hired buffalo herder
(Drawing in lecture Elementary Course)

> *"Wearing a big hat on your head is like a parasol. Holding a bamboo branch like a horsewhip, sitting high on a buffalo back, listening to the birds singing in the trees, watching butterflies fluttering in the grass. In the blue sky, the buffalo and you were relaxing and enjoying yourselves, thinking nothing was happier than that! This picturesque scene, set against the backdrop of nature's beauty, is the daily reality of a buffalo herder."*
>
> (Lecture Elementary Course)

However, the reality of buffalo herding is far from this idyllic picture. The buffalo herder's days are filled with constant vigilance, enduring rain, sun, mosquitoes, gadflies, and leeches. The buffalo leeches, in particular, are a constant threat, some resembling small, long worms that often crawl into buffalo ears. That is a testament to the cultural significance of buffalo herding in the Six Provinces (Lục Tỉnh), where the people have a saying that vividly captures the scene of mosquitoes and leeches:

> *"Mosquitoes make sounds like playing flute*
> *Leeches wade like sticky rice noodle soup."*

Even in the dead of night, the buffalo herder's work is still unfinished. They must often wake to light another fire and light a bow to ward off mosquitoes for the buffalo herd. The use of fire and the bow is a testament to the buffalo herder's ingenuity and resourcefulness. Straw is beaten into long strands like a braid, considered firewood, which is used to keep the fire alive (in the past,

A lagoon for the buffaloes to lie down is called a buffaloes swamp. (Lecture Elementary Course)

there were no lighters). It's also used to travel at night to replace lamps and repel mosquitoes for buffaloes, pigs, or other people.

During the season, when there are many mosquitoes, the buffaloes have to lie down in the lagoon, and in the morning, they have to take the buffaloes to bathe. The dew is cold, and the air is highly stinky.

Some stay as servants to herd buffaloes for their owners until they have a wife. The status of a buffaloes herder is both poor and ignorant. So when criticizing someone for being naive, people often say: "You are a buffalo herder." What a pity!

Reading the buffalo and the buffalo herdsman in the Lecture Elementary Course, we see the context of agricultural life in our countryside in the past. Rural life is very peaceful and simple, even though it is difficult how it used to be, how it is now. Between people and animals, the relationship is as close as human to human, like the following folk song:

> "O buffalo, I say this to buffalo,
> Buffalo let go out into the fields to plow with me.
> The plow is the capital of farmers,
> I am here, buffalo there, and we will manage the work.
> As long as the rice plant still blooms,
> There are still grass blades in the field for buffalo to eat."

Today, the sight of buffaloes in our country is a rarity. Farmers now plow, pull, and thresh rice with machines, a stark contrast to the past when these tasks were carried out with the help of these gentle giants. As Lenin prophesied, they have truly been 'liberated' from the toil of manual labor!

The image of the buffalo and the buffalo herder, once a vibrant part of our rural landscape, now exists only as a memory. The fields, once filled with the rhythmic plodding of buffalo hooves, now echo with the mechanical hum of tractors. This transformation is a poignant reminder of a bygone era, altering how we farm and the very fabric of our rural life. It's a loss that evokes nostalgia and contemplation about the changes in our agricultural practices.

4. MY VILLAGE

In the past, our people predominantly resided in the countryside, a landscape devoid of cities. This rural setting was a hub of activity, with people exchanging goods and products at the countryside market. The agricultural economy was a testament to our self-sufficiency and independence.

The Vietnamese village is the smallest basic administrative unit, but it is the basis of society and a gathering place for community activities. In addition to the administrative headquarters in the South called Nhà Việc (as in the US called Civic Center), that place also has a communal house and a pagoda.

All people's activities revolve around communal houses and pagodas. Every village in the South has a communal house. The communal house is the place to worship the village's gods. The sacred decoction given by the King is kept carefully in a wooden box kept by an elder. Every year at the temple worship festival, the new delicacy is brought back to the communal house for worship. The communal house was built by the village's common fund, the public fund, which is the fund for joint work (công nho, công nhu) and everyday needs. On the contrary, pagodas are built by individuals, and the monk comes to lead them.

The formation of Buddhism in the Southern region was unique. Unlike in other regions, there was no church. Instead, the wealthy individuals of the community took it upon themselves to build pagodas, seeking blessings and donating gardens and farmland to the pagoda for financial support.

Depending on the circumstances and conditions, pagodas and communal houses are erected, without a specific plan, and not necessarily clustered around the House of Worship. These communal spaces, in addition to their religious functions, also serve as the primary venues for resolving conflicts and addressing the emotional and legal issues of villagers. Despite the centralized feudalism of the ancient Vietnamese regime, the villages in Việt Nam enjoyed a unique autonomy, a stark contrast to the villages in Europe.

The King's laws were lost to the village rules.

That ancient folk saying speaks of the chracteristics of the villages. In the past, Việt Nam had a very high level of grassroots democracy. France came to rule and considered it a unique feature, maintaining it in the Southern region of France. Legal scholars also used that to write books and teach in Vietnamese law schools. In the Lecture Elementary Course of elementary class (first grade of village school), there is the article "My Village" which I would like to quote:

> *"My village is near the province. There are bamboo fences around the village. From the outside, you can't see the houses. At the beginning of the village, at the end of the village, there are brick gates.*[5]*"*

Village brick-gate. There are bamboo fences around the village. (Photo: Lecture Elementary Course)

The compilation group[1] depicted "my village" in the North, a concept that may seem peculiar to students from the Southern region of Six Provinces. The mention of a "bamboo bank[6]" may find its way into poetry and literature, but it's a foreign concept to the people of the Southern region. In the same way, the Vietnamese youth

---

5 The compilation groups composed of: Mr. Trần Trọng Kim, Nguyễn Văn Ngọc, Đặng Đình Phúc and Đỗ Thận.
6 Lũy: The land bank planted with bamboo as a fence.

of the 50s and 60s were drawn to themes like "the Seine River⁽⁷⁾" and "the yellow light of Gare Lyon" in Paris, France, which were not part of the Southern region's literary landscape.

It is the same in the case of the Literary Group Tự Lực (*Tự Lực Văn Đoàn*). Fortunately, when the "country became independent," Mr. Hoàng Xuân Hãn composed the first educational program; he included some works of Tự Lực Văn Đoàn in the High School program. The incident made the entire generation of Southern students think that there was also Ms. Loan or Mr.and Mrs. Phán in the Six Provinces! Society was not feudal in the ancient Southern region, so it was unnecessary to "break off" like Ms Loan did when she severed ties with her husband's family!

The article "My Village" in Lecture Elementary Course beautifully captures the tranquil and poetic essence of "My Village," a simple life that is etched in everyone's memory. It evokes a sense of peace and reflection. Please quote:

> "*In the village, most of the houses are thatched houses, a traditional architectural style that reflects the simplicity and harmony of rural life. Every home has a yard with a garden or a pond surrounded by a bamboo fence. Vegetables, potatoes, and other fruit trees are grown in the garden.*

---

7 The Seine River flows through Paris, Lyon train station in Paris, France.

A family lives in the village
(Drawing in Lecture Elementary Course)

"*Only the road running straight through the village is wide; the rest are narrow, winding paths.*"

At the end of the article "My Village," the author "summarizes" by saying:

Living in the village, showy in the country.

The purpose of the Lecture Elementary Course is to summarize every lesson by the author in one sentence to impress and educate students. The mindset of our Vietnamese people was indeed like that in the past, and it still exists today.

The village is a place to express feelings of attachment and mutuality; when in emergency "at night no fire no lights" joy, sadness, and misfortune, we are still together. Negative, evil, and immoral expressions cannot exist. Therefore, because "living in a village," everyone must be kind to each other, making the community and village prosperous and peaceful.

From the village, people reach out to the larger surrounding society to compete, strive for manhood, and contribute to the country. 'Staying in the country' is not just an idea; it's a duty. Paying the King's favor and the country's fortune with mourning will make a man noble. The word 'Sign' here does not mean being wealthy because of property, money, or land, but 'going for the country' is understood as contributing to paying back the country's debt and the King's gratitude. Therefore, people, especially Vietnamese who have left their homeland, feel responsible for contributing to the work of building the "homeland." Otherwise, life feels meaningless, like lifeless plants!

Fifty years later, re-reading Lecture Elementary Course, multiplying the article "My Village" with the sentence: How poignant it is to live in a village and a country, especially as you get older.

The value of the Lecture Elementary Course will forever remain in the hearts of our generation. In addition to memories of childhood, it also has high educational value to this day.

5. MY VILLAGE TEMPLE

The pagoda image made many impressions on the spiritual life of ancient Vietnamese people, especially in the countryside. It retained many deep, beautiful, lovely, and lasting memories in each of us.

Whether you are a Buddhist or not, the bustling but gentle image of village temples on the full moon, the first day of the lunar month, or New Year's Day is beautiful, attractive, and charismatic.

Because Buddhism through festivals has been deeply ingrained in life for a long time, it has become a custom of our Vietnamese people.

The article "**My Village Pagoda**" in the Lecture Elementary Course for Preparatory class students (second grade today) describes the scene of a pagoda in the countryside a century ago.

The village was the administrative base of Việt Nam during the French period, "led" by the Village Committee (*Ban Hội Tề*). They were selected from people who had learned the national and French and had money. The Village Committee can "self-govern" over the central government. The leading dignitaries in the Committee include the following:

- **Village Leader** (*Hương Cả*): the oldest and wealthiest person in the village, head of the Village Committee.

- **Village Manager** (*Hương Chủ*): Hương Cả's deputy

- **Village Master of Ceremony** (*Hương Giáo*): explaining rituals and customs.

- **Village Teacher** (*Hương Sư*): a person with the highest education in the village, working as an advisor in complex and complicated jobs, preserving good customs and traditions.

- **Village Supervisor** (*Hương Trưởng*): similar to Village Teacher (*Hương Sư*) but less important.

- **Village Advisor** (*Hương Chánh*): a judicial advisor with experience in the village, originally from Village Secretary (Hương Than) or Village Security (Hương Hao).

- **Village Secretary** (*Hương Thân*): in charge of paperwork and books, capable of explaining official dispatches sent to the village by higher authorities.

- **Village Security** (*Hương Hào*): in charge of security.

- **Village Police** (*Hương Quản*): in charge of general police in the village.

- **Village Ceremonial** Organizer (*Hương Lễ*): takes care of rituals and sacrifices.

- **Commune Head** (*Thôn Trưởng*, or *Lý Trưởng*): a person nominated by the Village Committee and accepted by the government, along with the Village Secretary (Hương Than) and Village Security (*Hương Hào*), issue a list book and a tax book. All three people above are responsible for legalizing documents. He must pass this Village Head position for several years to occupy a higher position.

- **Village Book-Keeper** (*Hương Bộ* or *Thú Bộ*): keeps the village's documents.

- **Clerk** (*Biện Lại*): The Clerk paid for by the village to help with the village positions.

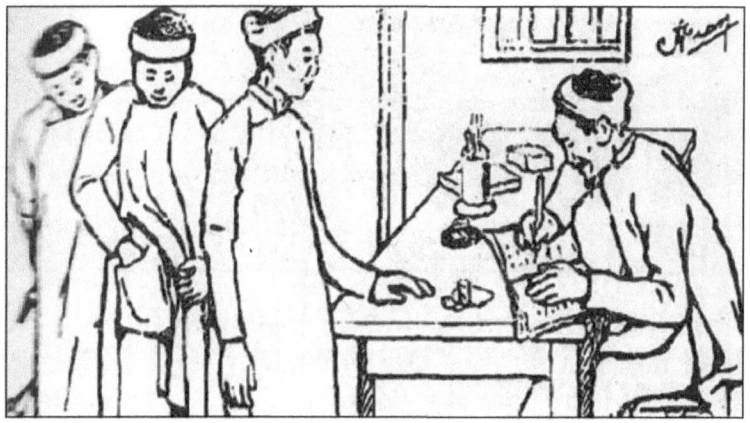

Villagers go to the commune chief's office to pay him taxes
(Drawing in Lecture Elementary Course)

Small positions such as **Boss** (*Trùm*), **Lead** (*Trưởng*), and **Security** (*Cai Tuần*) are the people who run paperwork and errands for the Village Committee.

The old Village Committee met and worked at Village Hall (Đình Làng). After the French came in, they built the Office to be the administrative headquarters of the commune.

(After "Việt Nam 1920-1945" of Ngô Văn, page 392)

Pagoda (or Temple) is a Buddhist facility built by private individuals in the village, so it does not belong to any leadership system. The monks look after everything with the villagers' material contributions.

That is a typical "my village temple":

> "My village's temple is roofed with tiles, in front there is a yard, on the side there is a pond, around there is a garden, in front of the yard there are three gates, above is the bell tower, below is the door to enter and exit.

The pagoda scene is generally a typical example of our pagoda in the countryside. (Drawing in Lecture Elementary

> *In the pagoda, on a high pedestal, are many painted and gilded wooden Buddha statues. Behind the pagoda is the ancestral house where the monks live. On both sides are guest houses. Outside the pagoda yard is a stone stele recording the merits of those who have contributed to the pagoda. Outside the garden, there are several towers where one of the monks who passed away is worshiped."*

The pagoda scene that Lecture Elementary Course describes above is generally a typical example of our pagoda in the countryside.

The pagoda is hidden in the countryside, with large, shady trees, far from the mundane. It always and forever expresses the spirit of Buddhism, especially Vietnamese Buddhism.

The three-entrance gate in front of the pagoda is not only a symbol of a pagoda but also a universal image, following a typical Vietnamese architectural style: It is seen in village communal houses and house gates from the street, mausoleums like Lăng Ông Bà Chiểu's tomb (also known as Tomb of the Marshal *Lê Văn Duyệt* in Bà Chiểu), Tomb of Mr. *Trương Vĩnh Ký*.

The three-entrance gate, with its three doors, symbolizes enlightenment and inclusivity. The main door, permanently closed, represents the separation from the secular world, while the two smaller doors, always open, welcome all: one for 'good men' (thiện nam) and one for 'faithful women' (tín nữ). This design does not imply that male Buddhists visit the temple out of kindness while female Buddhists visit out of faith. Instead, it signifies that the path to enlightenment is open to all, regardless of gender or social status. Understanding this symbolism can enlighten us about the inclusive nature of Buddhism and the architectural elements of our pagodas.

Because the temple doors are always open, anything that is "free." Thus, people call anything "free" as "temple's stuff." If you lose your way and stay overnight at the temple, if you're hungry or thirsty, go to the temple to eat a meal or ask for a drink of water for free. Eating for free is called "eating at the temple."

When did Buddhism come to our country?

Buddhism, a philosophy that had already taken root in India 500 years before Christianity, found its way to our country during the Giao Châu period at the end of the 2nd century and the beginning of the 3rd century. That marked a significant chapter in our history, as we embraced Northern Buddhism with Mahayana (Big Vehicle) from the north via China. Southern Buddhism entered from the south in the Thai-Laos-Myanmar direction, called Hinayana (Small Vehicle), similar to Theravada, the original Buddhism of India. The Giao Chau period, a time of cultural exchange and growth, connects us to our past and the roots of our beliefs.

In Vietnamese history, many Kings were devout Buddhists who chose monks as state teachers and advisors to the King. For example, King Đinh Tiên Hoàng (968-979) chose monk Khuông Việt as the Great Master (*Thái Sư*). Later, Vietnamese Buddhism flourished during the Lý Dynasty (10th century) and the Trần Dynasty (13th century).

Returning to the Lecture Elementary Course, the author described the scene of "My Village Temple" activities as follows:

> *On the full moon day and the first day, I often accompanied my grandmother to the Temple for the evening worship. The Monk would chant sutras, the sound of the wooden bell would resonate, and he would sit up there; my grandmother and the elders would sit below, engaged in worship and reciting Buddha's name. The bright candles on the table and the billowing incense smoke created a solemn and reverent atmosphere.*

As children, we would eagerly follow our grandmother to the Temple, often with the hope that the Monk would share some sticky rice or bananas with us and allow us to spend time with our friends. These visits to the Temple were not just about worship, but also about community and shared experiences.

Vietnamese Buddhism has no canon law that accepts very young children into the religion because Buddhism does not have a missionary agency like Rome.

In the past, Vietnamese people came to Buddhism no matter which way they came, but they were never forced because their minds and hearts wanted to go to Buddha, and learning about Buddhism was a need of Vietnamese people at that time.

As a child, I ate sticky rice and bananas at the temple. In the past, bananas were often offered at temples in my homeland. It is a type of Porcelain banana, also known as Siamese banana. Sometimes, people with money go to the pagoda with areca bananas, royal bananas, or sticky rice. Bananas are a native product in the South, easy to grow anywhere:

> *Summer winds bring dust after bananas tree,*
> *He loves his concubine and abandoned his children!*

I need to find out where the Southern people planted banana trees in front of their houses. Perhaps the name "banana" sounds unlucky, so people use it?

Banana trees are versatile. Porcelain banana leaves are used to wrap cakes and dry packages in market. Banh Tết, spring rolls, and spring rolls must be wrapped in banana leaves. Wrapping them in foil, like in Little Sàigòn, is not delicious and quickly spoils them.

Thin young banana stems are eaten skillfully with braised fish sauce. Old stems are chopped to feed to pigs or torn into small pieces to dry to make ropes for tying things or wrapping cakes.

Going to Pagodas is the happiest and busiest, becoming a festival during Tết. Talking about pagoda ceremonies, we remember the talented Poet and journalist Nguyễn Nhược Pháp. He wrote verses describing the scene of going to the Temple that are still so beautiful today:

I don't dare go fast
I'm afraid he'll judge me as too quickly
The destiny is toilsome, not prosperous.

Nguyễn Nhược Pháp was the son of Nguyễn Văn Vĩnh, born in 1914 in Hà Nội, died early at 24. Poetry collection, "Once Upon a Time," was published by Nguyễn Dương in 1935 in Hà Nội (as in Vietnamese Poet in 1941 by Hoài Thanh and Hoài Chân).

Every day, morning and evening, village temples come alive with elaborate rituals. The steady sound of the gong in the quiet night resonates with our souls each time we pass by the Temple, fostering a deep connection to our cultural traditions.

Thankfully, we are blessed with numerous magnificent, beautiful, majestic, and massive temples, along with other religious facilities, here in Little Sàigòn. However, the unique charm of 'My Village Temple' from our childhood, where we used to accompany our grandmothers to seek sticky rice and bananas, is a nostalgic memory we cherish dearly.

The elaborate sound of gongs and the monk's "My Village Temple" image belong to the past!

In Little Saigon, one night, when I passed by the pagoda, the electric lights were bright, but I did not hear the sound of elaborate gongs; instead, the sound of cars and singing came from the car someone had just driven in!

An early day of Ất Dậu Spring, 2005.

6. THE OLD-TIME SOLDIERS

People from ancient times knew how to live in groups in the form of tribes until civilization knew how to organize into nations, and there were often wars. Therefore, the compulsive soldiers appeared to protect (or invade) the tribe, territory, or country. The lesson "Old-day Compulsive Soldiers" was included by the authors of the Lecture Elementary Course in the Beginning Class and consisted of 2 parts:

Part 1: When leaving
Part 2: When staying in the guard station

Both were written as folk songs for students to learn by heart.

Part 1 describes the scene at the time of departure as follows:

"*His waist was tied with a yellow cloth belt,*[8]

---
8 *The belt is made of yellow cloth, worn around the waist.*

A grass hat⁽⁹²⁾ *on his head, a long gun on his shoulder*
One hand was holding an arquebus⁽¹⁰³⁾ *gun,*
One hand held a spear; the chief sent him on a boat
The drum beats five times at a time, continuously,
Stepping on the boat, tears fell like rain."

Soldiers here, the author refers to the compulsive soldiers of the past before the French entered; we can understand them as soldiers of the Nguyễn Dynasty. These brave men, depending on the needs of the commune and village, established a population listing book (for young men) in the commune and then selected 1 in 3 or 1 in 5 to hand over to the district official to transfer to the government to serve as 'compulsive soldiers' in the village. Localities or the royal court mobilized according to needs. Their bravery in the face of such responsibilities is truly admirable.

This article shows that our soldiers in ancient times had military equipment: yellow cloth belts around their waists, brass hats at the top, and arquebus long guns (which must be ignited to explode). The soldiers were still barefoot without shoes.

In the picture, we see soldiers' wives and children walking to the riverbank, holding their children in their arms. Meanwhile, the military mandarin had to beat

---

9 *The hat is made of leaves and has a brass top.*
10 *Fuze is used for top-loading (recharge) arquebus guns.*

Soldiers' wives and children walking to the riverbank, holding their children in their arms. The drum beats five times at a time, continuously, The soldier steps on the boat, tears fell like rain. (Drawing in Lecture Elementary Course)

the drum five times at a time, non-stop and ordered the soldiers to step on the boat to take them to a station far away, in the mountains and forests (a backward region). Those soldiers, leaving their families behind, made the ultimate sacrifice for their country.

What a sad parting scene! Our soldiers from ancient times were like that; how could they fight against Western soldiers with modern equipment, iron warships, and long-range guns? They had canons and were guided by Catholic Christians.

Reading the "Old-days soldiers," we can understand why Gia Định citadel was quickly lost; the three provinces of Biên Hòa, Gia Định, and Định Tường had to cede to France, as well as the last three provinces of the Southern region, Vĩnh Long, An Giang, Hà Tiên lost in 5 days!

Part two describes the scene at the guarding stations:

> "Three years of guarding the outposts,
> During the day, keep the watching spot; he took duties at night.
> Slashing (cutting) bamboo, chopping wood in the forests,
> Having a body that is having hardship, no complaints to anyone.
> The mouth eats bamboo shoots, apricot shoots,
> For those who are harsh and irritated, it's hard to make friends.
> The well's water is clear; the fish is flouncing."

In "Three Years of Defense," the author tells us that the military service regime at that time was three years; during this time, soldiers had to be sent far away to do post-guard duties. They are healthy people selected from communes and villages. There are still some older men or those whose families had to stay and work as local soldiers, such as village soldiers, insurgent soldiers, and

Three years of guarding the outposts
(Drawing in Lecture Elementary Course)

Part III
• COUNTRY AND PEOPLE

In the article shows the compulsive soldiers carrying trees to make barracks and guards. (Drawing in Lecture Elementary

civil defense soldiers, before 1975 in the Republic of Việt Nam.

The drawing in the article shows the compulsive soldiers carrying trees to make barracks and guards. Many soldiers were sent to work for the mandarins, perhaps as servants, serving the commander at their guarded station. Historically, administrative and military commanders were called mandarins, superior mandarins, prominent mandarins, district mandarins, province mandarins... When the French came to rule our country, they maintained that calling and had such detailed regulations. Which is an official, and which level is a big Mandarin? There are the Viet officials and French officials!

In contrast to the historical practice of addressing people as Mandarins, modern Việt Nam has adopted a more egalitarian approach, referring to individuals as 'sirs, ' a term that conveys a sense of civility and respect.

The status of our soldiers or American soldiers is the same. "Having bodies, having suffering." They don't know "who to complain to."

There was still a gap between soldiers and ordinary people during the old times of compulsive soldiers. But nowadays, the gap is enormous, so soldiers feel miserable.

Regular soldiers, conscripts, military duties, just different names, all aimed at calling healthy men to join the army. Depending on the military's purpose: Protecting the homeland, maintaining security, policing, protecting peace or invading, etc.

The authors in the Lecture Elementary Course do not mention the noble duty of our soldiers in the past or show what Western soldiers were like!

In the article "Compulsive Soldiers of the Past," the author only intended to tell a story: the soldiers of the past were like fairy tales. That is the purpose of the Lecture Elementary Course: non-political!

7. SIR PHAN THANH GIẢN

Lecture Elementary Course Preparatory class is a reading book (*Fr:* Lecture Cours Préparatoire) with 111 lessons. Although it is a reading book, it is highly educational. This elementary school textbook was used for half a century in the first decade of the 20th century.

Out of 111 articles, the authors devoted 10 to Vietnamese historical figures from the beginning to the present. As following:

1. The story of the Trưng sisters
2. The story of Mr. Ngô Quyền
3. King Lý Thái Tổ moved the capital to Hà Nội
4. Mr. Trần Quốc Tuấn
5. Mr. Lê Lai risked his life to save the lord
6. A rebel: Mạc Đăng Dung
7. King Lê Thánh Tôn
8. Mr. Nguyễn Kim

9. The Founder of the Nguyễn Dynasty: Mr. Nguyễn Hoàng

10. Mr. Phan Thanh Giản

Students are taught history through storytelling through reading exercises. That is a new method with high pedagogical value compared to when Việt Nam was under Western rule.

It was not easy for the authors to promote the character of Phan Thanh Giản in textbooks at that time if they did not have enough courage. They would never dare to do it if they did not respect Sir Phan Thanh Giản.

Let's read how the authors tell the story of Sir Phan Thanh Giản below:

"Sir Phan Thanh Giản was a Governor (Kinh Lược Sứ): a Mandarin with full authority to govern a region – three western provinces in South Việt Nam, namely Vĩnh Long, An Giang, and Tiên. When the French government attacked those three provinces, he knew they could not resist the French, so he ordered the city to surrender. But he wanted to show his loyalty to the King and punished himself for not being able to protect the province and country, so he drank poison and committed suicide."

Phan Thanh Giản is the first Doctor in the Southern region, a famous mandarin who served three generations of Kings: Minh Mạng, Thiệu Trị, and Tự Đức.

Sir Phan Thanh Giản was a Governor

Phan Thanh Giản was born in 1796 in Bảo Thạnh village, Ba Tri District, Bến Tre Province. He passed the Baccalaureate of the Gia Định school in 1825, the following year, 1826, the Doctor of the National Assembly exam (*thi Hội*), and was the only person to pass the Doctor at this course.

His Chinese ancestors fled the Manchu Qing (*Mãn Thanh*) Dynasty, went to Vĩnh Long (now Bến Tre) in Southern (*Đàng Trong*), and became the Minister of Law Department (*Thượng Thơ Bộ Hình*) in 1847 under King Thiệu Trị, then Minister of Administrative Department (*Thượng Thơ Bộ Lại*) in 1848 under King Tự Đức.

In reality, Phan Thanh Giản did not give the provinces to the French, as the Lecture Elementary Course recounts. Let's go back to Vietnamese history at that time:

In 1862, the situation in the Southern region became more urgent after the Kỳ Hòa garrison in Gia Định fell, and the French, in turn, occupied Biên Hòa, Thủ Dầu Một, Tây Ninh, Định Tường, and Bà Rịa. The Huế court sent Phan Thanh Giản and Lâm Duy Hiệp to Gia Định to negotiate peace. As a result, we had to sign the treaty on June 5, 1862. We ceded three eastern provinces to France: Biên Hòa, Gia Định and Định Tường. Next, he took over as Governor of Vĩnh Long and was ordered to negotiate with the French to save the situation.

In 1863, he was appointed Ambassador to France (*Như Tây Chánh Sứ*) with the hope of redeeming the three lost provinces. The Mission had to wait in France for over two months and, in the end, only received an empty promise, a bitter disappointment that weighed heavily on our nation.

France's ambition to occupy the remaining three provinces –Vĩnh Long, An Giang, and Hà Tiên – was approved. Tự Đức once again ordered Phan Thanh Giản to go to the South to find a way to deal with the situation. On June 20, 1867, Mr.Phan and Vĩnh Long's Police Officer Võ Doãn Thanh met with De Lagrandière to hold talks. France's demands were not just excessive; they were unjust. Our side requested to consult the Huế court; De Legrandiere approved.

Returning to the citadel, Phan Thanh Giản was met with the sight of the French army's occupation of Vĩnh Long citadel. Despite this, he continued his mission. Châu Đốc fell at midnight on the 21st and 22nd, and Hà Tiên on the morning of the 24th. In five days, three provinces were lost, and the entire territory of the southern region fell into the hands of pirates. His mission may have failed, but Phan Thanh Giản's unwavering determination was a testament to his love for his country.

After writing notes about the court and speaking about the country's unstoppable fate, his words were pitiful, advising his children not to collaborate with the French to try to support the King. Then, he starved for 17 days without dying. In the end, he had to drink poison and commit suicide, died on July 5, 1867. After his death, he was harshly impeached by the royal court, stripped of his position, and his name on the doctoral stele was erased. However, justice prevailed. It was not until Đồng Khánh, in 1886, that Phan Thanh Giản was restored to his previous title, a recognition long overdue.

However, the people of the South still respected him and built temples to worship him in Bến Tre, Vĩnh Long, and Trà Vinh. During the Republic of Việt Nam before 1975, his name was given to the street and school.

After 1975, the North Vietnamese Communists came to the South and erased temples and street names, burying the name of Phan Thanh Giản once again. Thinking carefully, we see that the famous Mandarin Phan Thanh Giản was born in a turbulent time. His personality and life were a "tragedy of the times."

Today, after 30 years, the Southern Việt Nam Communists have proven their integrity and seek to restore the honor of Sir Phan Thanh Giản.

The authors of the Lecture Elementary Course once had the audacity and love for Vietnamese history. Thus, the Lecture Elementary Course is a Textbook set with timeless value.

8. INDOCHINA RAILWAY

At that time, Indochina was the term used to refer to five French colonial countries: the Southern region, the Central region, the Northern region, Cambodia, and Laos. Sometimes, it is also called the French Indochina Federation.

Following the French occupation of Indochina, the region became a focal point of colonial exploitation, often under the guise of 'sowing civilization.' That was manifested in the construction of steel wire houses, tap water systems, schools, markets, and transportation networks, which significantly altered the local landscape and way of life.

Establishing the Indochina railway was a pivotal part of the colonial exploitation program, serving as a vital tool in the French's efforts to 'sow civilization.'

The introduction of trains in the North was a significant departure from traditional modes of transportation, a fact kept from the people of the time. The author of the Lecture Elementary Course, designed for students of Prep and Second grade at village schools, had to emphasize this point: '*The train line runs throughout Indochina...*'

After humans discovered the circle, they invented the wheel that rolls on the ground, reducing friction. That was a great revolution.

In my homeland, in the past, farmers pulled rice seedlings and pulled rice in the fields with "barrows" and "paddles" (children pull and play in the yard with areca sticks or coconut leaves), so it is cumbersome and complex because of friction.

Tracing the history of vehicles in our country, we see a progression from

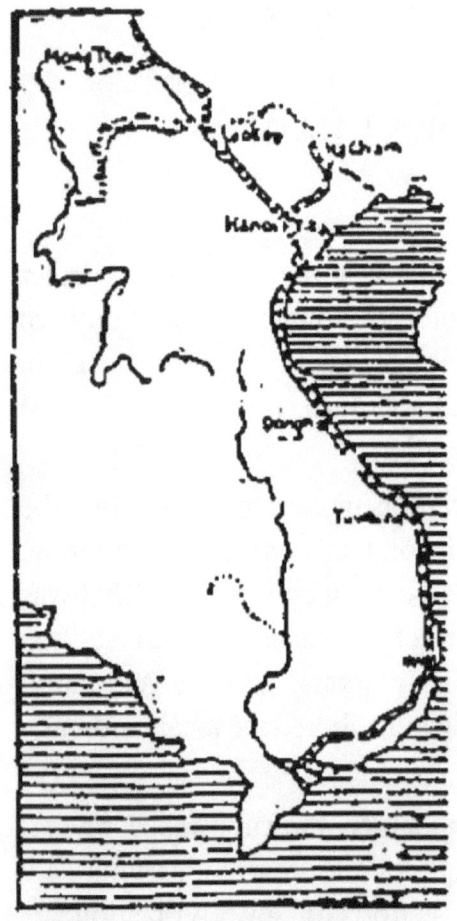

The train line runs throughout Indochina is a failed project.
(Lecture Elementary Course)

Part III
• COUNTRY AND PEOPLE   291

horse carts, ox carts, and buffalo carts (pulled by animals) to rickshaws, buggies, and cyclos (pulled by people). This evolution culminated in the introduction of vehicles powered by machines such as cyclos, mobilities, and Honda, etc.

All images of human-drawn carts, horse-drawn carts, or tractors have certainly created many impressions and memories of the lives of Vietnamese people for generations of Vietnamese people.

In Lecture Elementary Course, the opening lesson, *The Railway Runs throughout Indochina*, the author writes:

> *"In Indochina, the French have laid out many train lines to carry passengers and goods; now those lines have passed through rich places and farmers."*

When did trains exist in Việt Nam? And what is the history of the Indochina railway?

- According to documents, in 1879, Mr. Thévenet, Director of the Southern Region Public Works Department, followed the orders of the Governor of the Southern region at that time, Le Myre de Vilers (the name of the first Nguyễn Đình Chiểu High School was Le Myre de Vilers), establishing the Southern region railway project.

The Southern Region County Board approved this first train project in Việt Nam with nine votes in favor and five votes against it after 6 hours of debate on

November 22, 1880. That is a historic day for our Việt Nam train system.

Le Myre de Vilers' project plans to build a railway starting from Sài Gòn through cities in Six Provinces to Châu Đốc in Việt Nam, then to Nam Vang (Cambodia), Vạn Tượng (Laos), and finally to Yunnan (China). The leading country (France) did not approve the plan because the trade route to Yunnan had already been opened through the Hồng Hà River in the northern region.

In the end, the Indochina train project failed, so France only allowed the establishment of the Sàigòn - Mỹ Tho railway as a test for establishing the Indochina train later. The Sàigòn - Mỹ Tho train route has become history, opening the door to the train system throughout Việt Nam.

Trains from Saigon arrive at the station in Mỹ Tho.
(Drawing in Lecture Elementary Course)

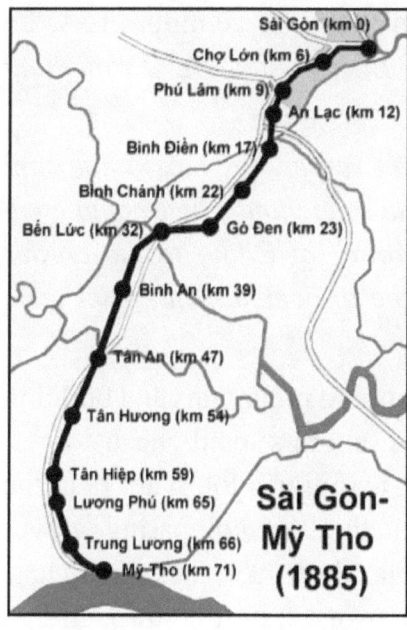

The people of Mỹ Tho certainly cannot forget the image of a vast iron train, belching smoke and honking loudly, running through the peaceful Vòng Nhỏ area every day in the past!

Do you know? That road started construction in November 1881 at a cost of 11.6 million Francs and first rolled on July 20, 1885. At that time, the train bridge Bến Lức over Vàm Cỏ Đông had yet to be built, so passengers had to change buses. By May 1886, the new train ran throughout Sàigòn-Mỹ Tho, 71 km long through the stations of Sàigòn, An Đông, Phú Lâm, An Lạc, Bình Điền, Bình Chánh, Gò Đen, Bến Lức, Bình Thạnh, Tân An, Tân Hương, Tân Hiệp, Lương Phú, Trung Lương, and Mỹ Tho. The places the train passed through must have created many exciting and attractive images for Vietnamese people.

Then, in 1958, Mr. Ngô Đình Diệm decided to abolish the Sàigòn - Mỹ Tho railway after 73 years of operation, which caused a great stir in the hearts of the people of Mỹ Tho and the South at that time!

The Lecture Elementary Course continues to write about the article *The Railway Running Throughout Indochina* as follows:

> *"Among those train routes, the most important one runs throughout Indochina. Once completed, places from the border of China to the border of Siam will be able to communicate with each other."*

While exploiting forests and mountains and building railways, the French used laborers, paid cheap wages, lived in poverty, got sick, and died a lot. After that, the French introduced the method of comparing graves to encourage poor people. Just like the Americans, when they opened the east-west train line through San Francisco, they also used the policy of hiring labor from China, which still has many historical traces.

Đà Nẵng train station
(Drawing in Lecture Elementary Course)

Le Myre de Vilers' train project was later replaced by the trans-Việt Nam train project, which is still in use today: it runs from Sàigòn-Huế đến Hà Nội and then to Yunnan (China).

> *"Currently, the first two sections have been completed: one section to the North from Na Sầm to Cửa Hàn, one section from Nha Trang to Sàigòn. But until the whole road is completed, cars will transport passengers from Nha Trang to Cửa Hàn and from Sàigòn to Siam. So from North to South, it doesn't take much time; on one side, it only takes two and a half days."*

(Lecture Elementary Course)

The article *"The railway running throughout Indochina"* was written in the early twentieth century. At that time, the road was not yet completed. However, things did not happen as planned later.

The train stops at the station to pick up passengers to board. (Drawing in Lecture Elementary Course)

The train stops at Huế passenger station
(Drawing in Lecture Elementary Course)

At that time, traveling by train from North to South took two and a half days, which was too fast, beyond one's imagination (now it takes only two days).

The trans-Việt Nam train route mainly ran along Mandarin Road, once the King's Road was used for military and official work. It pushes back the image of our sovereignty to the past, replacing it with a protection regime. However, objectively speaking, the train system has contributed to changing the face of Việt Nam from a material to a spiritual life.

Meanwhile, in urban areas such as Sàigòn, Mỹ Tho, Cần Thơ, Hà Nội... The French have changed the face of the cities from the image of horse-drawn carriages to human carriages. The jingling and "clinking" sounds of the tomb cart or glass cart are replaced by the panting sounds of the rickshaw puller.

In 1888, France imported 400 hand-pulling carts (called rickshaws – *xe kéo*) into Sàigòn to serve the powerful class, and the horse-pulling carriages were taken outside the city.

Then, in 1934, a French official improved the human hand-pulling cart to look like a slave. The pedaled cyclo first entered Nam Vang, then passed through Sàigòn, and then to Bạc Liêu. Pedicabs are called "French cyclos" (*xích lô đạp*) by some people. The driver sat in the back, considered more polite and civilized, less of an enslaved person!

Vietnamese people improved hand-pulling carts and cyclos into multi-purpose "pedicabs" (*xe lôi đạp*). They carried people and goods on many terrains, in dark streets

Xe lôi đạp, "pedicabs," first appeared in Việt Nam in 1917 in Gò Công province, invented by the Gò Công people.

and alleys, reducing women's struggle and liberating the shoulders of Vietnamese mothers and sisters.

The bicycle tows a big box with two wheels attached to the back of the saddle, so it is called a "pulling cart." Xe lôi, or "pedicabs," first appeared in Việt Nam in 1917 in Gò Công province, invented by the Gò Công people. By the time there were two-wheeled motorbikes, the "motorcycle" replaced the bicycle pulling the trunk, called the "motorized buggy." It is simply called the buggy to distinguish it from the still popular "pedal buggy."

Besides "civilizations," backwardness has existed for a long time because many people at that time still drank river water and well water, used oil lamps, pulled carts, and rode cyclos.

The car's history, From handcarts to the Indochina train system, also shows progress.

Now, having the opportunity to return to the country, visit the countryside, and visit places that the Sàigòn-Mỹ Tho train passes every day is truly interesting and reminds us of mixed sadness and joy. Sitting on a cyclo or walking around the Sàigòn area, a bit of sorrow arises as if regretting a time gone by and what has been lost.

And is that mood only applicable to people living far away from home?

9. SÀI GÒN CITY

"Sàigòn is the largest port in Indochina. That city is on the banks of the Sàigòn River, with two creeks flowing on both sides, railways, roads, and especially waterways, that is, branches of the Mekong River (Cửu Long), Đồng Nai River, and many other canals, channels provide communication with other provinces and Cambodia."

(Lecture Elementary Course)

At that time, Sàigòn was the only port city of the five French Indochina countries, while Chợ Lớn and Gia Định were two provinces of the Southern region.

When the French first occupied Sàigòn, they destroyed Qui Thành (Gia Định citadel) so that people would no longer remember the royal relics. It also planned to change the name of Gia Định province to

Bà Chiểu or Tân Định, but due to people's reaction, the name Gia Định remained until 1975.

Sàigòn City developed due to its favorable geographical and economic factors, so it was called the *"Pearl of the Far East"* by Asian and European countries at that time.

Sàigòn is a commercial center that converges peoples, cultures, and religions worldwide. Here, the two civilizations of East and West meet, making Sàigòn people dynamic, outspoken, straightforward, brave, intelligent, open, and accessible to accept new things.

The two creeks running on both sides of Sàigòn are the Bến Nghé and Chợ Lớn canals.

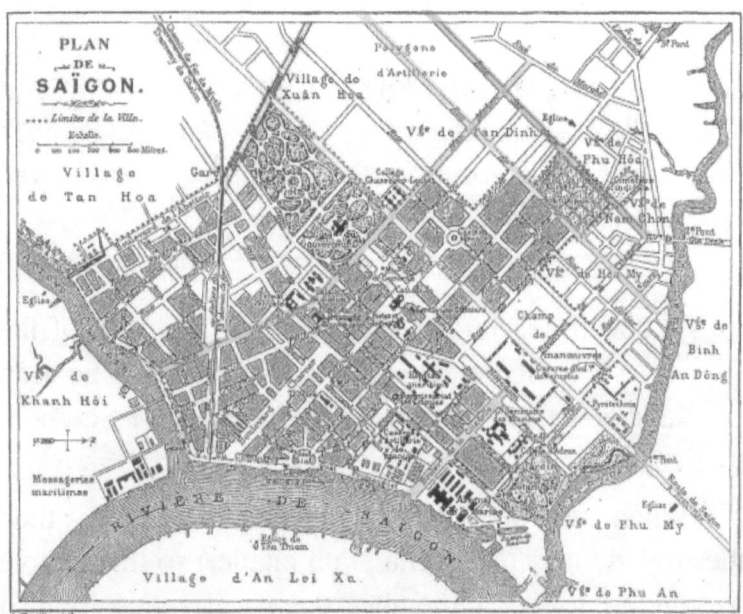

Map of Saigon during the French colonial period

The ancient Chợ Lớn canal was dry, so King Gia Long ordered dredging in 1819. The person in charge of the project was Huỳnh Công Lý, father-in-law of King Minh Mạng, who at that time was Deputy Governor of Gia Định and later was punished and beheaded by General Lê Văn Duyệt, Governor of Gia Định.

After digging the Chợ Lớn canal, King Gia Long renamed it An Thông Hạ, but the people still called it Kinh Tàu Hủ. Both sides of the Tàu Hủ Canal are the area of Chợ Lớn, Chinese people. They combined with the Singaporean Chinese, specializing in rice trading, transporting rice from the Six Province region, milling it, and exporting it. Today, it is Bình Đông station.

This area was formed around 1778 at the same time as the Chinese area in Cù Lao Phố, Biên Hòa. The Tây Sơn army once hunted it down and almost destroyed it because it followed Lord Nguyễn!

Speaking of Sàigòn City, we remember Mr. Nguyễn Hữu Cảnh, the founder of Sàigòn. In 1698, Lord Nguyễn Phước Chu (1691-1725) appointed Nguyễn Hữu Cảnh as Governor to invade the capital of Chân Lạp. He had the merit of establishing Dinh Trấn Biên or Biên Hòa, and Dinh Phiên Trấn or Sàigòn.

He recruited over 40,000 people, expanded Sàigòn by 1,000 miles, and established the Minh Hương commune for Chinese people in Phiên Trấn (present-day *Chợ Lớn*) and the Thanh Hà commune for Chinese people in Trấn Biên (*Cù Lao Phố*).

Regarding the life of ancient Sàigòn city, the Lecture Elementary Course describes:

> *"There are many ships, barges, and boats carrying rice grains from South Việt Nam to Chợ Lớn, bringing it to rice mills for milling and pounding, and then transporting it to Sàigòn station for export. Outside the harbor, there are transformer ships. Fled to North Việt Nam, China, Japan, Siam, the Philippines, the Indonesian archipelago, France, and other European countries."*

Sàigòn is 1,730 km away from Hà Nội by road and 50 km from the Pacific Oceanir. It is the largest port in Việt Nam to date, with an operating capacity of 10 million tons annually.

Saigon pier, 1868

Sàigòn has the railway developed very early, connected to many other prominent cities-first, the Sàigòn-Mỹ Tho line and then the Sàigòn-Huế-Hà Nội line. The train line in the inner city is the Sàigòn-Chợ Lớn train line, which people call the Middle Train line, running from Trần Hưng Đạo Street to Đồng Khánh Street.

In the past, rice grains from Six Provinces were brought to Bình Đông station, milled into rice, and then sold to the North or exported abroad, monopolized by Chợ Lớn Chinese traders. This policy dates back to the reign of Mạc Cửu.

At that time, the Chinese established a system of purchasing rice grains, building tents to grind rice, and

A drawing of Saigon harbor

pounding rice by hand, and they exclusively supplied it to Lord Nguyễn. Then, after the General Governor of Gia Định Lê Văn Duyệt continued to give the Minh Hương Chinese a monopoly until the French occupied Sàigòn, and then under Mr. Nguyễn Văn Thiệu, the Chinese also continued to get rich on the sweat and tears of the people of Six Provinces.

Lecture Elementary Course tells us that the Chinese exported rice to North Việt Nam, China, Japan, Siam, the Philippines, Indonesia, and Europe at that time.

Thus, at that time, Sàigòn was the largest urban area of the Six Provinces Southern region. Bến Thành market was built around 1859 when the French had not yet occupied Sàigòn. The market is located next to Qui Thành (Gia Định Citadel), next to the bank of Bến Nghé River, so it is called Bến Thành market because there are vehicles above and boats below On both sides, there are busy tiled streets where people trade all kinds of goods and a place to exchange goods with foreign countries.

After the French occupied Gia Định, they established a new "Market House" in today's Old Market (*Chợ Cũ*) area. Then, in 1887-1888, the canal in front of the market was filled in to create the quarter of Võ Di Nguy, Tôn Thất Thiệp, Nguyễn Huệ and Tôn Thất Thiệp, which is still very popular now.

Then, Sàigòn Market (*Bến Thành*) moved to its current location. Construction started in May 1912, and an opening ceremony was held in March 1914 for three

Administrative building in the center of Saigon city
(Post card)

An area in Cho Lon city
(Drawing in LIFE magazine)

days, 28, 29, and 30, attracting over 100,000 people to watch pleasantly. Thus, the old Bến Thành market became the current Chợ Cũ Market, and the New Bến Thành market was called New Market Sàigòn, which Sàigòn people also call Bến Thành market.

Despite numerous transformations, the Bến Thành Market has retained its original charm, with its iconic four-sided clock tower that overlooks the four market gates: East, West, South, and North.

The Bến Thành Market is a bustling hub of activity, housing over 3,000 shops that offer a wide range of products, from everyday necessities to gourmet delights and luxury items.

Anyone, younger or older, who has a chance to revisit Sàigòn cannot help but stop by Bến Thành Market to enjoy a familiar dish and remember a specific memory.

New Sàigòn Market (Chợ Bến Thành) at its current location

Or maybe we have time to drive past, look at the clock tower, look at the Quách Thị Trang roundabout, and then go to Tân Sơn Nhứt airport to return to the United States, bringing with us a little bit of Sàigòn to hurt and miss less!

Sàigòn symbolizes the Sàigòn people, the Southerners, and also friends and relatives living abroad!

Since 1975, Sàigòn has changed its name!

Despite the upheaval of name changes and the shifting of roads, the people of Sàigòn remained true to their nature: daring, brave, and resilient. Their spirit of survival and adaptability rose above the turmoil, a testament to their strength.

Sàigòn is proud to be the first place to popularize and develop the national language, the first place to publish the Nhựt Trình newspaper for people to read, the leading place in economics, culture, and art, and the place with a team of intellectuals. Following Mr. Đồ Chiểu:

> *Carrying so many ethical ones, but the boat still handles it,*
> *Stabbing some evil guys, and the pen is not worn.*

Sàigòn people are proud to have contributed over 30% of the country's total GDP, accounting for 1/3 of foreign investment projects and revenue reaching 1/3 of the country's total revenue today.

Sàigòn has cultural, educational, and religious works associated with people in the South, overseas, and now the whole country. These include Pétrus Ký High

School, Gia Long High School, Tao Đàn Garden, Zoo, Ông Bà Chiểu Mausoleum, Giác Lâm Ancient Pagoda, Post Office, New Chợ Lớn, Independence Palace, and Notre Dame Cathedral.

Sàigòn has existed for over 300 years.

Over its 300-year existence, Sàigòn has developed a unique lifestyle that defines its people. From their culinary preferences to their fashion choices, leisure activities, and reading habits, the 'Sàigòn people' have a distinct way of life.

Today, our eating habits are more than just a routine; they're a culinary culture. The food of the ancient Saigon people has not only left a strong impression but has significantly shaped our culinary lives today, even overseas. We owe much of our culinary heritage to the ancient Saigon people, a legacy we should deeply appreciate and respect.

Let's explore a fascinating example of a Saigon menu that the Đồng Nai newspaper recommended in 1932. This menu, a testament to Saigon's rich and diverse culinary traditions, offers a variety of dishes that will pique your interest. It's not just a menu but a historical document that reflects the tastes and preferences of the Saigon people of that era and how these have evolved.

Breakfast: white porridge served with one of the dishes: fried braised fish, added a little water, and then braised until crisp. Or eat dried shrimp fried with onions or snakehead fish floss and radishes soaked in fish sauce.

- **Lunch:** Mint and sour soup, grilled fish (river or sea fish), pork intestines stir-fried with onions and vermicelli (vermicelli).

Boiled vegetables (amaranth shoots or sweet potato shoots). Meat braised in coconut milk.

- **Dinner:** meat soup cooked with mustard greens, meat braised in coconut water (left over at noon), sauerkraut or bean sprouts, sliced fish or perch salted and fried, crab stir-fried with vinegar.

You can eat like that forever or change to unique meals if bored. Let's delve into the exceptional and diverse flavors of Saigonese cuisine. Each dish is a distinct culinary journey, offering a new perspective on the local culture and traditions.

For breakfast, indulge in the variety of Saigonese cuisine, from bean porridge with braised snakehead fish and pepper, a dish that symbolizes the harmony of flavors, to broken rice with grilled pork ribs, a staple dish showcasing the Saigonese people.

- **For lunch**, try gourd soup cooked with yellow catfish; beef stir-fried with water celery, snakehead fish braised with boiled, thinly sliced pineapple heads, or yam soup. Or try sour pineapple soup cooked with braised salty fish and sliced fish and meat. Braised salty fish is also eaten with water-spinach, various raw vegetables, and chili. It goes with alum fish soup and braised sea bass.

- **For dinner**, Try luffa soup with lean meat and fish sauce boiled in water, which must be mixed with duck eggs. Banana pods or eggplants (short and round eggplants) are also eaten raw with fish sauce, bitter melon soup, and meat stew.

In brief, for over 300 years, the people of Saigon have crafted a unique identity – the Saigon identity. This identity, born in the South, was embraced by the entire region and became a part of the national consciousness post-1975. The evolution of this unique cultural identity, a testament to Saigon's rich history and cultural significance, is a story waiting to be explored by those interested in Vietnamese culture, inviting them to be part of this larger community.

Lunch of a working family in Saigon
(Drawing in LIFE magazine)

Even with the city's name change, Saigon people continue to embody the essence of Saigon, proudly referring to their town as Saigon and cherishing their identity as Saigonese.

Horse-drawn carriages were a common means of transport in Saigon in the past. (Post Cart)

Saigon river boat wharf (Post Cart)

Saigon symbolizes adaptability and openness. Once hailed as the **Pearl of the Far East *(Hòn Ngọc Viễn Đông)***, its people are always open to new experiences and embody the spirit of freedom and self-mastery. The resilience and progressive spirit of the Saigonese people, who have thrived in the face of adversity and change, are truly inspiring. Their ability to adapt and unwavering optimism in the face of challenges is a testament to the human spirit.

Now, rereading the article "Saigon City" in the Lecture Elementary Course, I see that none of us are a little proud, whether we were born or raised in Saigon. Why?

Saigon has thrived in the face of adversity and change, representing its people's spirit of resilience and optimism. The progressive nature of the Saigonese people symbolizes Inspiration and Hope.

A painting of the Saigon riverbank in 1929

10. LITERATURE AND POETRY IS NOT GOOD

Lecture Elementary Course used it as a memorization lesson for elementary school students in the past. *"Literature and poetry is not good"* is the opening sentence of the article *"Advice to go back to farming,"* a folk song genre:

> *"Literature and poetry is not good,*
> *Return to the old village to learn how to plow.*
> *Every morning, I carry a hoe and visit the fields,*
> *Water runs out, I grab a hanged bucket and slap it up.*
> *Out of the newly-grown rice plants, I carry them more,*
> *Out of plants, I'll bring money to buy some rice barrels.*
> *Later, when good rice plants grow full of the field,*

They will spend time to harvest, thresh, and plow."

This poem, a popular piece of literature, serves as a powerful didactic tool, guiding and supporting students in their learning journey about the value of farming and the work of the rice cultivator on the field. It was particularly aimed at elementary school students who struggled with literature and poetry, encouraging them to appreciate the cultivation process.

This folk poem nicely describes the job of a rice cultivator in a historical context: watering the field with the individual hanging buckets, planting the young rice plants, buying the new plants and seeds stored in the barrels, and pouring rice into the barrel. It's a glimpse into the past that helps us understand the evolution of farming practices. At the time, the French government made metal rice barrels of 40 liters as a measuring tool.

Carry the hoe to visit the fields
(Drawing in Lecture Elementary Course)

When good rice plants grow full in the field, farmers spend time plowing, harvesting, and threshing to obtain good rice.

At the time, 'agricultural encouragement' articles, including this piece, were familiar to most elementary students. These articles provided valuable advice for farmers and effectively showcased their past work.

Planting and plowing are the capital of farmers.

Plowing, as the primary step in agriculture, plays a crucial role. It aims to break up the soil, turn it over to make it loose, and kill the grass. The depth of plowing directly impacts the quality of the future rice, hence the saying:

Plow deeply and hoe carefully.

Our people learned the technique of using buffaloes to plow fields very early. In the North, one buffalo is often used to pull the plow, while in the Six Provinces, two buffaloes are used.

Cultivating is hereditary. It was an old custom for a student who felt unsuitable to follow the literary path to return to the village to follow his father or his brothers to learn how to plow and farm. That was an ordinary story, and they felt good being good farmers.

The process of using buffaloes for plowing is quite intricate. A slightly curved piece of wood, known as a yoke, is hung on the necks of a pair of buffaloes. A driving rod running vertically between the two buffaloes connects this yoke to the plow, allowing the buffaloes to pull the plow.

For a buffalo to be tamed, it must practice plowing with its owner for at least two seasons. This dedication is mirrored in the hard work of people and animals from dawn until sunset before resting. The saying "as toiled as a buffalo" originates from this.

The image of a yoke on the neck of a pair of buffaloes was used to represent human hardship as well as the slavery of people during the Chinese and Western rule periods:

- *Yoke in the middle of the way; wear it around the neck.*
- *Foreign domination yoke*

After preparing to plow and harrow, which involves checking the condition of the soil, repairing any farming tools, and ensuring the buffaloes are in good health, it's time to plant.

Seed rice is selected from the previous season and kept carefully in jars or roofs. In ancient times, jars and

A buffalo to be tamed, it must practice plowing with its owner for at least two seasons. (Lecture Elementary Course)

roofs were ubiquitous. Everyone needed them, from the royal court to the ordinary people, and used them to store water, dry food, rice, sticky rice, etc.

The image of a young girl, on a moonlit night, scooping buckets of water from the bathing jar behind the sidewalk, next to the banana bushes and bamboo groves, or the image of people walking on the street on a hot summer afternoon, stopping by a pot of water in front of someone's alley, scooping up a bucket of rainwater, drinking hastily... the result is stunning, the beauty of the peaceful old days in our homeland.

They used the same jars to soak the rice seeds. The seeds were soaked for one night and one day, taken out, and incubated until they became succulent, which required careful monitoring and patience. Then, they were sown into seedlings. This meticulous and patient process was a fundamental part of traditional rice farming.

Soaking seeds and sowing rice seedlings was a task reserved for the skilled hands of experienced farmers. Their expertise and dedication were crucial to the success of the farming process.

On the other hand, the field hands were responsible for cultivating rice, watering, and hoeing grass, each playing a crucial role in the traditional farming process.

In Six Provinces, there are places where the weather is still sweltering until the fifth month of the lunar calendar. Occasionally, there are some early rains of the season, which farmers eagerly await and call 'defoliating rain.' These rains help the leaves of the rice plants fall off, making it easier for the farmers to harvest the rice, a moment of great relief and anticipation.

During the (lunar) Fifth month, the weather harms humans and animals. At that time, we worshipped on the fifth lunar day of the fifth month to ward off weather diseases. The fifth day of the fifth lunar month is also known as Tết Đoan Ngọ or the Mid-year Festival. According to divination books, the Ngọ spiritual place is in the South, belongs to the positive hexagram, and causes the hot air.

In those days, people collected medicinal leaves such as lemon grass and marjoram leaves to bring home and cook for the whole family to bathe in to prevent diseases. Some people even prepare medicinal leaves in advance, dry them, and save them. Some places also have specially prepared herbal remedies used on this occasion to prevent malaria, cold, stomachache, and diarrhea, which are passed down as precious medicines. Bathing in medicinal herbs is a folk experience that has been around for thousands of years and has long become a custom of our people during the Half-Year Festival.

In Chợ Lớn or other places where Vietnamese people interact with Chinese people, on May 5 (lunar year), the Festival or "Tết" Đoan Ngọ, there are more fruits and feasts to offer. "Tết" Đoan Ngọ is the moment the sun is closest to the earth, and this day is often "The middle day of summer" (Summer Solstice – Hạ chí). In Việt Nam, this day is also the death anniversary of the National Mother Âu Cơ, a Deity.

People often offer bamboo leaf rice cakes, ash water rice cakes, and fruits. Some places even cook bean porridge and then eat it to cool down. After the offering, the whole family eats together after bathing in the water of fragrant leaves, called medicinal leaves, with the hope and belief that the entire family will be healthy that year and no one will get sick from the weather!

Returning to the rhythm of farming work, the farmer gently tends to the water in the field after transplanting, nurturing the rice for a bountiful harvest. Rice fertilizers and pesticides were not as prevalent in the past as they are today, reflecting a more straightforward, more natural approach to farming. This simplicity brings a sense of tranquility and a peaceful coexistence with nature.

Then, when the northern wind blew gently, the rice fields started turning yellow, a sight that signified the approaching harvest season. In the cold weather, people went to the fields to cut early-ripened sticky rice flowers with red tails. The seeds, still soft and with some milk, were returned to the village. They were washed, dried, and pounded in a large mortar with a heavy pestle. The mixture was then dried, creating the beloved flat rice flakes.

The echo of the pestle stirring green rice under the moonlight, the young men in the village gathered around the young girls, some grated coconut, others scraped rice husks, then mixed the rice grains with grated coconut and granulated sugar, and there was a flat bowl of green rice. This communal preparation, filled with laughter and shared tasks, not only adds a unique warmth to the dish but also fosters a sense of belonging and warmth in the community.

Today, re-reading the article "*Advice to go back to farming*" in the Lecture Elementary Course, I remembered the old days, the new rice cooker, and Chợ Đào rice, eaten with yam soup.

The rice harvest season at the end of the year is also the preparation season for Tết, reminiscent of the sound of a pestle rubbing puffed rice cakes, remembering the image of the brand new cotton mats covered with puffed rice cakes lying in the sun drying in front of the yard, next to piles of rice.

"The rich literature is not good,
Return to the old village to learn how to plow."

The rice harvest season at the end of the year is also the preparation season for Tết. (Painting)

Living with fields and gardens, farmers feel happy and happy from generation to generation, creating a peaceful and leisurely landscape in the countryside.

> *Hey, don't leave the fields fallow,*
> *How many inches of land, that many inches of gold!*

Whether scholars or farmers, our people have always loved their fields and gardens and taught their children to value the rice grain, seeing it as God's pearl.

The article "Advice to go back to farming" reflects the spirit of loving hard work and respecting farmers with muddy hands and feet, which was the morality of our people in the past.

Hey, don't leave the fields fallow,
How many inches of land, that many inches of gold!

11. THANK HEAVEN FOR TIMELY SUN AND RAIN

Our people's concept of 'Heaven' is a rich tapestry woven with diverse threads of interpretation. It is simple and sublime, inviting us to explore its many facets.

Our people think the word "Heaven" is rich, diverse, simple, yet sublime.

First of all, Heaven refers to the vast space above your head, also called the Sky; as the saying goes:

- *The Sky is high, and the earth is wide*

- *The Sky is high, and the sea is vast,*
  How to live to fulfill our love as husband and wife

Heaven is also often used to refer to the supreme being, master of all things, master of human destiny, such as:

> - Buddha and God
> - Oh, my old God.
> - Why is the God not fair,
>   Some have three or four wives; some have no wives.
>
> - Oh my God, why do you create the enemy?
>   It is causing my husband to go to war.

In the Vietnamese language, Heaven refers to the weather, rain, sunshine, drought, and floods.

> - When it rains, the potato leaves get wet.
>   He's been working on it for two long years.
>
> - It's raining, and the balloons are heaving,
>   Mom gets married; who will I live with?
>
> - It's raining, wet with dust, wet banks,
>   Wet trees and wet leaves
>
> - Who would have thought it would be wet for me?

In the Lecture Elementary Course, the lesson "Plowing" is used as a memorization lesson for Preparatory class students. In it, the author talks about "Thank God."

> "Thank God, it rains and shines when it's right,
> Some places are harrowed shallowly,
> and some places are plowed deeply.
> The labor doesn't mind taking a long time,
> Today, the country is silver; the next day, rice is golden.

Please don't leave the fields fallow,
How many feet underground, yellow feet much."

The word Heaven often refers to a divine being and also to a weather phenomenon that is very familiar in folklore, especially in the lives of farmers in our country in the past.

Our people's belief in a Supreme God controlling the elements was deeply ingrained in ancient times. The King's annual offerings to Heaven were not just a ritual but a profound expression of faith and hope for 'good weather' and a peaceful country, a testament to the farmers' deep-rooted beliefs.

A farmer's work is challenging and takes a lot of effort, and that's why the Lecture Elementary Course says:

"*Justice doesn't last long.*"

Despite the economic nature of farm work not aligning with today's society's standards, it was a collective family effort in rural areas. The husband, wife, and children all contributed to the labor, emphasizing the shared responsibility and commitment integral to their way of life and the strength of their familial bonds.

The greatest happiness of ancient farmers is waiting for the harvest, reaping, and bringing rice home. Deciding "success or failure, win or lose," the farmer entrusts himself to God because God brings rain and water. So, to this day, there is still a saying:

First water,
Second fertilizer,
Third, diligence,
Fourth, seeds.

The water and sky elements are still factors that determine life and death. Besides, our people in the past only worked in the fields for one season. If the harvest

failed, the whole family would be hungry all year, so they had to borrow rice to eat, waiting for the next season!

> *"Today, the silver water; tomorrow, the golden rice."*

Silver water is water covered with copper white, and water is also silver, meaning money, to turn the hard work of cultivating into "golden rice."

How precious a grain of rice was to our grandparents in the past.

In the South, the word "silver water" refers to the water season that flows from Nam Vang to the river Tiền and river Hậu in the Fifth and Sixth months of the lunar calendar. At that time, the fish Linh arrived, changing the face of the rural areas bordering the Southwest.

Part III
• COUNTRY AND PEOPLE

Today, the country is silver; the next day, rice is golden.

It is said that the land of the South is generous, so the season of "cultivation" of heaven and earth gives people here many "exotic delicacies," making visitors from faraway regions bewildered, even if they only taste it once.

Speaking of the fish *Linh*, according to Mr. Nguyễn Văn Hầu in the book *"Half a Month in Thất Sơn Region,"* in the flood season, the fish *Linh* has just hatched its babies, wandering around the border to Đồng Tháp Mười to River Tiền; from Láng Linh to river Hậu. From then on, the small fish flow into rivers and canals and onto the fields. Then, in October and November of the lunar calendar, the "big" fish *Linh* flows into the big river to provide people with delicious and nutritious meals.

You can go right with the dish of braised slightly salty fish marinated with tamarind or fish Linh braised in a hotpot with salty fish sauce and served with flowers Điên điển. It is incredible!

Particularly in Gò Công, you can also savor the fish Linh dish, a culinary delight cooked in sour flower soup with flower *So Đũa*, dipped in salty minced shrimp, and savored with fresh rice. This dish, with its unique blend of flavors, including the tanginess of the sour soup, the freshness of the fish, the saltiness of the shrimp, and the nuttiness of the rice, is a testament to the region's rich culinary heritage. Enjoy it to your heart's content, and you'll be pleasantly surprised by its deliciousness!

Though the sour soup with fish *Linh* and flowers *So đũa* is a copy of the sour soup with fish *Linh* and flowers *Điên điển*, they have become an essential part of our people's diet, and it continues to be so. This dish carries a rich historical context, a connection to our past that we are proud to share with you.

> *Please do not leave the fields uncultivated.*
> *How many inches of land, that many inches of gold!*

Since ancient times, our Kings have implemented agricultural promotion policies, instructing local areas not to leave fields uncultivated.

However, when Lord Nguyễn expanded the territory into what we now know as **Phương Nam**, the fields and lands became scattered, and there was a shortage of workers, so people had to be brought in from the central region. Individuals who clear or cultivate land would be granted ownership rights and exempt from paying the district's tax (in the form of rice) for ten years. Therefore, Mr Đồ Chiểu's *Oration for the Righteous Soldiers of Cần Giuộc* begins with the following:

> *"Oh my!*
> *The enemy's guns thundered, revealing the people's hearts.*
> *After ten years to break the field, it's unlikely that you'll still be famous. Like an insurgent battle against the French, even though the sound is like a gong."*

If you don't understand the reclamation policy, you won't comprehend what Mr Đồ Chiểu meant by saying, "Ten years of work to break the field." This phrase symbolizes [specific historical or cultural significance], a vital aspect of the reclamation policy during that time.

In the Six Provinces, not only did we farm, but our ancestors also knew how to grow crops and fruit trees as a primary occupation, now called specialized farming. That is seed growing (growing vegetables, mustard greens, melons, onions, corn, beans, and eggplants on high ground) and planting fruit trees, established betel, areca, guava, and banana gardens.

Having the opportunity to visit Bến Tre and Cù Lao Bảo, Cù Lao Minh, and Cù Lao An Hóa, rice fields mixed with coconut gardens full of fruits, only to see all the efforts of our grandparents over many generations to leave over forty thousand acres of Coconut trees to this country as today.

Or visit Cái Mơn, the homeland of the Six Provinces' unique durian fruits. The initiative to create techniques for grafting and hybridizing fruit trees and ornamental plants has helped over 6,000 families live freely and leisurely in the fields and countryside.

With salty water and acidic soil in the countryside of Gò Công, the ancients knew how to choose suitable trees and get rich without working hard in the fields. Gò Công has round-fruited custard apple trees (called *quả Na* in the North). The locals call them sea custard apples or chewy custard apples. Sea custard apple has a vibrant, sweet, yet salty taste, chewy segments, and few seeds. It is considered a high-class fruit grown on sandy coastal soil.

Then, in the last three decades, Gò Công grew strange plants again, having fun and making real money. That is the fruits "Gò Công's cherries," with the name proving that the copyright has been certified by the land of Gò Công.

Therefore, in Six Provinces, before the French entered, people knew how to take advantage of river and sea estuaries as a place for trade and exchange and turned that place into a commercial port. These are Nông Nại, a great trading port in Biên Hòa, Bình Đông trading port (Chợ Lớn today), Mỹ Tho Old Market Street trading port, Hà Tiên trading port, especially in Bãi Xàu, Sóc Trăng, which is a rice trading center. Rice exported to China (not to Saigon) existed before the 18th century.

For a time, Bãi Xàu Port traded with foreign countries. In addition to rice, chickens, ducks, pigs, and fruits were exchanged for Chinese fabrics, dishes, and traditional Chinese medicine. Bãi Xàu is the commercial center of Six Provinces of Vietnamese, Chinese, and Khmer people, creating a unique cultural feature that remains to this day through the relics of Vietnamese communal houses, Chinese pagodas, and Khmer pagodas.

Re-reading the lesson on plowing in the Lecture Elementary Course shows the hardship of our ancestors who worked hard in the fields. It also explains the feelings and emotions between ancient people, the gods, and the sacred being collectively called Heaven.

The East and the French diverge in their interpretations of Heaven and Earth. In our belief system, a profound connection exists between Heaven and Man, governed by an invisible yet omnipresent law known as Tao, the Tao of Heaven.

Could this unique understanding of Heaven and Earth have instilled in our clan an enduring optimism and love for life, enabling us to triumph over numerous historical challenges over the past 4,000 years?

The golden rice season is the joy of farmers

REFERENCES

1- Trần Trọng Kim- Nguyễn Văn Ngọc- Đặng Đình Phúc - Đỗ Thận, *Lecture Elementary Course, Việt Nam Tiểu Học Tùng Thư* 1948, NXB Trẻ in lại 1996

2- Trần Trọng Kim, *History of Việt Nam, Việt Nam Sử Lược*, NXB Đà Nẵng in lại 2003

3- Trần Quốc Vượng, Vũ Tuấn Sáng, *Thousands of Years Old Hanoi, Hà Nội Nghìn Xưa*, NXB Hà Nội 1998

4- Vương Hồng Sển, *Saigon Years Old, Sàigòn Năm Xưa*, NXB Tp. HCM 1990

5- Sơn Nam, *Mekong Delta*, Đồng Bằng Sông Cửu Long, NXB Xuân Thu in lại

6- Dương Quảng Hàm, *Essentials of Vietnamese Literature and History, Việt Nam Văn Học Sử Yếu*, NXB Sống Mới 1979

7- Nhất Thanh, *Land in the Countryside, Đất Lề Quê Thói*, NXB Tp.HCM 1992

8- Sơn Nam, *History of the Southern Desolation, Lịch Sử Khẩn Hoang Miền Nam*, NXB Văn Nghệ Tp.HCM 1994

9- Huỳnh Minh,

- *Gò Công Past and Present, Gò Công Xưa và Nay*, tác giả xuất bản, 1968

- *Dinh Tuong Past and Present, Định Tường Xưa và Nay*, tác giả xuất bản, không ghi năm

- *Vĩnh Long Past and Present, Vĩnh Long Xưa và Nay*, NXB Thanh Niên, 2002

- *Bac Lieu Past and Present, Bạc Liêu Xưa và Nay*, NXB Bách Việt, 1994

10. Nguyễn Hiến Lê, *7 Days in Đồng Tháp, 7 Ngày Trong Đồng Tháp*, NXB Xuân Thu 1954

11. Phạm Cao Tùng, *Polite People, Người Lịch Sự*, NXB Đại Nam 1951, reprinted by Da Nang Publishing House in 2003

CONTENTS

Preface • Love And Truth: Message of The Book   9

Appreciations:

NGUYỄN VĂN SÂM • The Book "Love And Trust In The Textbooks" and the writer's feelings about a lost time   19

PHẠM CAO DƯƠNG • A Title for "Love And Trust In The Textbooks"   25

PART I
ETHIC TEACHING TEXTBOOKS

1. Study And Practice Hard To Become A Person   31
2. What Is A Familial Clan?   38
3. Brothers Are Like Arms And Feet   44
4. Being Grateful To Your Parents   53
5. Obey Your Parents   61
6. Respect Your Parents   68

7. Love Your Parents	75
8. Ancestors Worship	81
9. Choose Your Friend Wisely	92
10. Death Anniversary	101
11. History Of The Country	108
12. Love Others As Loving Yourself	120
13. Near Mud But Not Stink Of Mud	127

PART II
FAMILY AND SCHOOL

1. Go To School On Time	137
2. As A Person You Have To Go To School	141
3. What Is The Purpose Of Going To School?	149
4. Students Are Grateful To Teachers	155
5. Strong Will Of A Man	161
6. Must Keep Your Heart Pure	171
7. My Homeland Is The Most Beautiful	176
8. A Delicious Meal	191
9. Grandma Lulls Her Grandchild	197
10. One Who Goes, One Who Stays	207
11. Going To The Market To Pay	215
12. Soggy Rain And Chilly Wind	225

PART III
COUNTRY AND PEOPLE

1. Education In The Past	235
2. Year-Round Agriculture Work	244
3 The Buffalo	252
4. My Village	261
5. My Village Temple	267
6. The Old-Time Soldiers	277
7. Sir Phan Thanh Giản	283
8. Indochina Railway	289
9. Sàigòn City	299
10. Literature And Poetry Is Not Good	313
11. Thank Heaven For Timely Sun And Rain	322

AUTHOR
SƠN NAM TRẦN VĂN CHI

PUBLISHED BOOKS:

1- *Understand the Vietnamese Cải Lương Opera - Tìm Hiểu Cải Lương.* Văn Mới published in 2005.
2- *Flavor of the Old Days – Hương Vị Ngày Xưa -* Xưa Và Nay published in 2005, republish in 2006 and 2024
3- *Haven of Love and Truth - Tình Nghĩa Giáo Khoa Thư.* Xưa Và Nay published in 2005. republish in 2006 and 2024
4- *Trần Văn Chi, Activities in U.S.A. - Trần Văn Chi, Hoạt Động tại Hoa Kỳ.* Đông Á published in 2001
5- *Haven of Love and Truth* (Version English) SỐNG Publishing, 2024

UPCOMING BOOK:

- *Good Morning Little Sàigòn*

NAM SƠN TRẦN VĂN CHI

Tình Nghĩa Giáo Khoa Thư

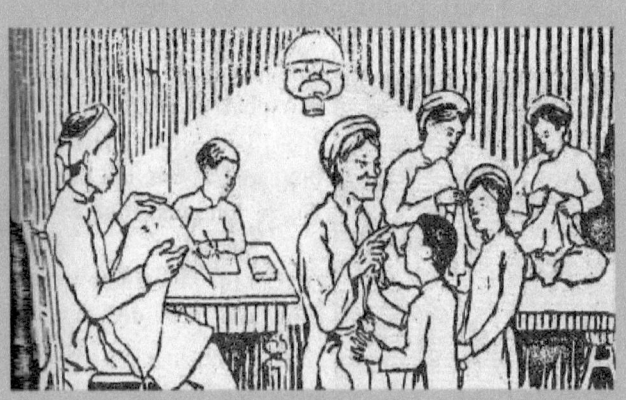

Song Publishing
2024

Nam Sơn Trần Văn Chi

Translator **Huyền Trí**

HAVEN of LOVE and TRUTH

SỐNG Publishing, 2024

NAM SƠN TRẦN VĂN CHI

Triều Nguyễn và Công Cuộc Mở Đất Phương Nam

Song Publishing
2024

NAM SƠN TRẦN VĂN CHI

HƯƠNG VỊ NGÀY XƯA
và MÓN NGON MIỀN NAM

Song Publishing
2024

www.ingramcontent.com/pod-product-compliance
Lightning Source LLC
LaVergne TN
LVHW041744060526
838201LV00046B/905